The White House

Gardens and Grounds

White House Landscapes

White House Landscapes

Horticultural Achievements of American Presidents

Barbara McEwan

Walker and Company
New York

First published in the United States of America in 1992 by Walker Publishing Company, Inc.

Published simultaneously in Canada by Thomas Allen & Son Canada, Limited, Markham, Ontario

Library of Congress Cataloging-in-Publication Data
McEwan, Barbara.
White House landscapes : horticultural achievements of American presidents / Barbara McEwan.
p.   cm.
Includes bibliographical references and index.
ISBN 0-8027-1192-8
1. Presidents—United States.   2. Horticulture—United States—History.   3. White House Gardens (Washington, D.C.)   I. Title.
E.176.1.M427   1992
973'.099—dc20   91-41081
CIP

Endpaper map by Kathy Kirby
Frontispiece illustration courtesy of the Library of Congress

Book design by Shelli Rosen

Excerpts from letters of George Washington to John Beale Bordley and Arthur Young on pages 3 and 4 reprinted from *American Gardens in The Eighteenth Century: "For Use or for Delight,"* by Ann Leighton (Amherst: Univ. of Massachusetts Press, 1986), Copyright © 1976 by Isadore Leighton Luce Smith, © renewed 1986 by Emily Smith Cain.

Printed in the United States of America

1   2   3   4   5   6   7   8   9   10

CONTENTS

ACKNOWLEDGMENTS

I wish to thank the following for their contributions to this volume.

Bill Flemer III, Princeton Nurseries, Princeton, New Jersey, for a gracious foreword.

Dr. James L. Owens, Professor of History, Lynchburg College, Lynchburg, Virginia, for reviewing the historical content in the midst of term papers and final exams.

Mary K. Knill, archivist, Lyndon Baines Johnson Library, Austin, Texas, for researching various aspects of the contributions by LBJ and Lady Bird Johnson to the White House grounds and elsewhere.

Lisa B. Auel, curator, exhibits branch, National Archives, Washington, D.C., for assistance in locating photographs of the White House grounds.

Mary Kennan Herbert, my editor at Walker and Company, who provided helpful editorial guidance.

LIST OF ILLUSTRATIONS

Although the grounds of the White House in Washington, D.C., are one of the most fascinating gardens in this country, they are relatively little known, even to the gardening public. Small portions of them frequently appear on television news spots, but the really interesting parts are very rarely seen. The perfectly kept lawns and east and west gardens are a credit to the special section of the National Park Service charged with their maintenance. However the unique features of what can truly be called our national garden are the splendid trees and the interesting histories connected with them.

The White House grounds must be kept closed to the general public for obvious security reasons. When portions are opened for special ceremonial occasions, the public cannot roam at will, and only special tours for small groups of horticultural enthusiasts can present an intimate glimpse of the plant treasuries growing there. Barbara McEwan's book is a very welcome addition to the rather scant literature on this large park that is so central to our national history and that of the many presidents who took a deep interest in its development and refinement. It was not an easy book to write because there has not been an ongoing and complete history of the grounds from the late eighteenth century to the present time. Rather, there have been sporadic records of developments made by the long sequence of presidents and the subsequent changes accomplished in later administrations. Some of the foremost American landscape architects and planners were involved in drawing up and modifying landscape plans culminating in the grounds that exist today. As McEwan states, there is little likelihood that the present layout will be changed materially. An ongoing process will be the replacement of aged trees like the John Quincy Adams elm on the south lawn, which only recently died.

The book unfolds the fascinating evolution of what was originally called the President's Park into the White House grounds of today. It is almost impossible to imagine the rustic and rural area in which the original White House was built. The muddy roads were little more than wagon tracks and livestock roamed at large, trampling through the unfenced grounds. McEwan recounts in important detail the background of the early presidents, all of whom were farmers, but on a scale that gave them the leisure and means to develop their properties as gentlemen's estates. Furthermore they were exceptionally well educated men, well read in the up-to-date horticulture of their eras, and in the case of Thomas Jefferson, widely traveled abroad with ample opportunity to see firsthand the great estates and gardens overseas. This book provides a detailed account of the development of the early presidents' own domains, with the ever-present threat of exhaustion of the soil and the first serious attempts to restore its fertility, an entirely new concept in the young country.

Although much is known about the development of Mt. Vernon and Monticello, relatively little has been written about the farms and estates of the later presidents and their contributions to the evolution of the White House grounds. Still less is known about the professional gardeners and managers who were hired and in some cases made a career of the management of the White House gardens, men like Charles Bizet, John Ousley,

Jemmy Mayer, and John Watt. No traces remain today of the large greenhouses that were once a prominent feature on the grounds, and it is hard to realize how big and impressive they were and what a large portion of the total maintenance funds were consumed in their operation. An important feature of this book are the illustrations of the White House and its grounds from early versions to the present. Of particular interest are the exterior and interior views of the greenhouses and the once elaborate flower beds on the north front of the White House.

As a member of the White House Grounds Committee of the American Association of Nurserymen, I am particularly glad that this book has been published. It greatly adds to our perspective and counsel of today to have such a clear history of the evolution of this fascinating park and grounds, a living link with the affection and interest that such a long sequence of exceptional men took in the White House landscapes.

William Flemer III, Princeton Nurseries

Biographies of presidents usually concentrate on their politics. This book focuses on what chief executives (and in some cases their wives) have done to improve the White House grounds.

Of our forty presidents to date, at least eighteen showed more than a casual interest in the acres surrounding the executive mansion. Those of us who notice trees, shrubs, and flowers owe a great debt to this group, because in virtually every case when something beyond ordinary grounds maintenance was done, it was due to the direct involvement of the president himself. Perhaps this is as it should be. The White House, despite its public nature, has always been considered the President's House. Congress has appropriated money (seldom enough, and many times grudgingly) for both interior and exterior preservation and renovation, but the couple in residence have been surprisingly free to determine how the money is spent.

In the case of Lucy Hayes, because she loved flowers, $1.00 of every $4.00 appropriated for the maintenance of the White House went to the glasshouses. Edith Kermit Roosevelt was not so fortunate. With the White House in extremis in terms of the need to restructure the by then old, much-used mansion, she sadly if voluntarily forewent a small but elegant greenhouse to replace those architect Charles F. McKim was tearing down in her husband Theodore's term. The budget, she decided, would not allow for such a facility.

Even though each president interested in the appearance of

the White House grounds had access to the most talented professionals in America, it is interesting how freely most of them offered—or insisted on—their own ideas of what should be done. This was because almost without exception they came to the office well prepared in the horticultural department. John Quincy Adams did not begin a serious interest in the subject until he was elected president, and Martin Van Buren did not learn the pleasures of growing plants until after he left office. Some presidents, such as George Washington and Thomas Jefferson, made significant contributions to horticulture before becoming chief executive, and several other occupants of the White House, most notably Jefferson, James Madison, and Lady Bird Johnson, made noteworthy contributions to some phase of botany after residing in Washington.

Our earliest presidents (Washington through Andrew Jackson, except for John Quincy Adams) were primarily farmers by occupation, as were most of their fellow citizens. Later presidents interested in landscaping almost without exception also came from a rural background. Agriculture and horticulture have much in common, and the farming experience at some period of their lives seems to have been the basis for the interest of almost all American presidents who took an active role in landscaping their homes and, later, the White House.

But by the early 1900s America literally extended from sea to shining sea, and farming gave way to industry and service jobs for increasing numbers of citizens—including future presidents. Therefore over the years horticulture has generally assumed less of a role at the White House than it once did except for several presidential wives who loved flowers and aggressively promoted their cause.

The presidents, for their part, have been more aware of the fact as our population has grown, so has grown the necessity for conserving the plants and animals the United States was blessed with at the time of our nation's founding. In this century the three presidents genuinely interested in the outdoors (Theodore Roosevelt, Franklin Delano Roosevelt, Lyndon B. Johnson) therefore distinguished themselves not as hands-on gardeners but as promoters of environmental causes. FDR's total renovation of the White House grounds—which alone would have ensured him his place among the botanical luminaries of the mansion—is in retrospect eclipsed by his environmental activities. By LBJ's time, the design of the grounds was well established. Future presidents may redesign gardens within their present locations—as, for example, did John F. Kennedy—but it seems unlikely there will be any further major changes to the President's Park.

White House
Landscapes

George Washington
1789-97

Like almost all his peers, George Washington was first and foremost a farmer, one of the most conscientious of any era. For most Americans in Washington's day, farming was a necessity. In Virginia, except for speculating in lands to the west (which Washington engaged in) and the slave trade (which he did not), money was difficult to acquire without being a tobacco planter. For some, such as Washington, farming was also adopted from the conviction that minding plants provided a gratification impossible to attain in other occupations. While he had happily spent a portion of his life as a surveyor and a soldier, this period was during his young manhood, before his marriage in 1759 to the wealthy young widow Martha Custis.

Through his wife, Washington acquired tobacco plantations on the York River. These complemented the plantation of Mt. Vernon, which had been owned by his half-brother Lawrence until his death. Beginning in 1754, George then leased the estate from Lawrence's widow, and upon her death in 1761 the estate became his. Unfortunately Mt. Vernon had been much neglected for years, and when George resigned his military commission at the end of 1758—just in time for his marriage the following January—the young man, age twenty-six, had his work cut out for him. Fortunately the Custis plantations had been ably managed and continued to be so by steward Joseph Valentine until Valentine's death in 1771. Bullskin, another major plantation in the Shenandoah Valley (in what is now Jefferson County, West Virginia), which Washington had bought in 1750, was leased to tenants, as was the case with other properties he owned. Thus from 1759 until 1775, when he assumed command of the Continental Army, Washington had an opportunity, albeit interrupted by his service in political capacities, to improve his knowledge of plants and running large estates.

In tune with his times Washington understood the importance of sheer numbers of acres to his financial success, not only for speculative purposes but also to satisfy the appetite of tobacco for virgin soils. In anticipation of Mt. Vernon's ultimately being his, he therefore added 172 acres to the original tract of 2,126 acres the year he signed the lease with his sister-in-law. By the time Mt. Vernon was legally his, he had bought almost 3,000 additional acres. He continued to buy property in the vicinity through 1786, and he ultimately held more than 7,000 acres. These he divided into 5 independently managed farms. Only the Mansion House farm does he seem to have kept for himself to manage.

He was fortunate he could put these earlier years to good use. From 1775 to 1783, the war years, he was able to visit his home only twice. The presidential years (1789–97) took another enormous portion out of his life as a farmer. Indeed, from 1759, the year he married, to 1799, when he died, approximately half of this time was spent away from Mt. Vernon in fulfillment of his duty to his country. The lure of the soil at his plantations made his decision to assume command of the American forces against the British and especially his agreement to two terms as president a unique example of self-sacrifice to one's country. He said with conviction, "I can truly say I had rather be at Mount Vernon with a friend or two about than to be attended at the Seat of Government by the Officers of State and the Representatives of every Power in Europe."[1]

While Washington loved his creature comforts, and a high social standing was ever his goal, it would be incorrect to assume that his agricultural efforts were for his benefit alone. A 1788 letter to John Beale Bordley, who owned on the Chesapeake a 1,600-acre tract that he ran as an agricultural experiment station, shows well Washington's sense of obligation in this field. "Agriculture being my favourite amusement," he wrote, "I am always pleased with communications that relate to it. . . . Experiments must be made, and the practice of such of them as are useful must be introduced by Gentlemen who have leisure and abilities to devise and wherewithal to hazard something. The common farmer will not depart from the *old* road 'till the *new* one is made so plain and easy that he is sure it cannot be mistaken."[2] After Washington became a farmer he worked tirelessly to determine how to make agriculture succeed in his part of the country.

He received deep satisfaction from his labors. To the English agricultural writer Arthur Young he observed, "Agriculture has ever been among the most favored of my amusements, though I never have possessed much skill in the art, and nine years' total inattention to it has added nothing to a knowledge, which is best understood from practice; but, with the means you have been so obliging as to furnish me, I shall return to it, though rather late in the day, with more alacrity than ever."[3]

Today the visitor to Mt. Vernon is still impressed by the mansion and the landscaped grounds, as were Washington's own guests. Evidence of the farming activities that made the estate viable is gone, given modern population pressures in the area. Nevertheless, because of their importance to Washington's pocketbook and his abilities as a landscaper, they should be explored first.

Washington was very much a product of his age. He inherited both ambition and soils depleted from abuse. From 1619, when John Rolfe shipped the first barrels of tobacco (four in number) from Jamestown to England, Virginia was dominated by this one crop. Everyone grew it, from the very poorest (often to the exclusion of food) to the man who had already known the trappings of the rich. It became the crop that could enrich a person's bank account within a few years. Men who could never dream of becoming well-to-do in England found tobacco a most obliging plant in America. It soon provided the standard against which its planter could judge himself and be judged.

To Washington's everlasting mortification, he never personally mastered the art of growing the weed. This was not because he didn't try; throughout his life Washington was driven by a desire to excel. From the earliest entries of his diary we know that he relied on tobacco to pay for imported goods from England so it is evident that his wife's plantations were most important to his finances. Yet in this period, tobacco planters—Washington among them—were for a variety of reasons switching to wheat. He found that Mt. Vernon land responded well to the grain, and, just as important, the market abroad held up throughout his lifetime.

He would have been an enthusiastic farmer in any case. The range of his field crops went far beyond tobacco, wheat, and the mandatory corn. They included alfalfa, potatoes, hemp, flax, Jerusalem artichokes, field peas, and hop clover, among some sixty others. Hemp and flax were necessary for manufacturing clothing for his people. Artichokes and potatoes were fed to livestock. As for the legumes, he understood their value in increasing the fertility of his soils.

Washington, however, was motivated beyond mere utility. Despite his military and political activities he found time and energy to plan and conduct numerous farming experiments. He saw clearly that farm practices had to be changed if American agriculture were to continue for generations. Even in his lifetime the trend was toward settlement to the west. This was due in large part because tidewater soils had been depleted because of the constant planting of tobacco. Farmers who switched to alternating wheat and corn succeeded briefly, only to find that this schedule finished off what fertility was left. Thousands of acres went back to pine and scrub, and desperate men and women moved on.

It remained to Edmund Ruffin, America's first soil scientist, who began his work in Virginia after the War of 1812, to show that this apparent loss of fertility was due to the soil's acidity, which effectively locked up nutrients. Meanwhile, progressive farmers like Washington, few in number but determined nonetheless, tried various possible remedies. One of these he experimented with, marl, was on the right track in terms of making the soil less acidic. The remainder demonstrate the range of possibilities. Washington used animal manure, green manures, and mud from the bottom of the nearby Potomac River. He tried each alone and in combination with other ingredients as per his own recipe for compost.

Washington tried various crops to see which did well in his particular soils. He experimented with drilling seed as opposed to broadcasting it and varied the application rates. He changed the distances between rows and tried the Native American method of interplanting, using peas and potatoes between this corn rows instead of the Native Americans' beans and squash. He went one step further and by 1788 had laid out a series of tables for crop rotations for each field. A plan covering a period of more than three years was a new concept here. The term itself dates only from 1778, just a decade before Washington records practicing this method. One rotation plan he made out, for example, provided for corn and potatoes the first year, then wheat, buckwheat for "green" manure, another year of wheat, followed by three years of clover or grass. Washington then calculated the number of days needed to plow, the dates involved, the expected quantity to be harvested and its value, and left room for an evaluation of the results.

Jefferson is famous for his record keeping of his gardening and farming activities. Washington's was even more thorough, and his records demonstrate a complete grasp of detail as well as the overall picture of his farming operations. In his farm instructions of 1768, for example, each farm and each field within each farm are treated separately. More important, unlike Jefferson's, Washington's bookkeeping was quite a model, although it did nothing to prevent him from spending lavishly on imported goods even when he knew his income did not justify it, at least in the short term. Yet Washington knew his profit or loss at each farm. Just as important, he was mindful of small expenditures—such as the cost of an overseer's keeping a horse, an expense he felt unjustified.

Like Jefferson, Washington sought additional means of increasing his income. Possibilities included few methods. His mill was one. By 1765 he was planting hemp and flax, which he hoped might add to his cash supply as well as clothe his slaves. The river running past his door (the Potomac) held marketable schools of shad and herring, and in 1765 he had some of his workers begin making a suitable schooner to catch them. Distilling his fruit supply beyond his personal needs was also feasible. Each of these endeavors, however, brought problems of their own, and he never made much money from them.

Serious plantsman as he was and familiar with the design of large estates elsewhere, Washington naturally turned his thoughts beyond agriculture to the beautification of his own property. In this he had no help from a professional landscaper, there being none in America at that time. He did have three assets. First, his years as a surveyor had trained his eye well in judging distances. Second, he studied books on landscaping and observed the landscaping of his American contemporaries. Third was his own innate sense of design, without which the first two assets would not have produced the results at Mt. Vernon.

Not surprisingly, the greatest periods of productivity with his landscaping occurred during the periods he was at home, when he could personally lay out beds, tree groupings, lawn areas, and walks and drives and supervise the plantings and construction. For such elaborate plans he relied on others at his peril.

The first major planting period occurred after his marriage in January 1759. Washington was determined to make Mt. Vernon a showpiece. Although he had yet to become the legal owner of it, as long as he kept up his lease payments of tobacco, the estate would ultimately be his. His second great good fortune was the fact that from 1759 to 1775 he was able to live the life of a private planter interrupted only by public service of his choice. Thus he had the time to establish the basic plan that visitors to the estate see today. But the authenticity of the reconstructed areas was made possible mainly because of his English friend Samuel Vaughan, who had made a scale drawing of the area west of the house during a six-day visit in 1787. Upon receiving the drawing (he had not been at home during Vaughan's stay) Washington found only one error in its execution. Additional plantings were made after the Englishman's visit, but the stage itself was set.

Washington had been faced with the dilemma of all great plantation owners. His house, his major jewel, had to be set off to the best advantage. Yet in the self-sufficient plantation of the pre– Civil War period, outbuildings were essential to the functioning of the owner and his family. A wash house and a laundry yard were a close second to the urgent need for a building for a kitchen. These were supplemented by a salt house, a smoke house, and an ice house. Garden areas were essential for providing food for the master's table. These in turn required a gardener, who needed housing for himself and his tools. The horses needed for transportation also had to be located reasonably close to the house. This necessitated a stable, a paddock, and a coach house. The overseer and house slaves, in order to be most effective, had to similarly be quartered along with their tools and other equipment near the center of their responsibilities. The basic question was how to screen off these dependencies so they would not detract from the mansion, yet arrange them for the greatest convenience.

With the Potomac at his door, Washington had both his greatest asset and his greatest liability. That he was satisfied with his solution can be seen in his later placement of the White House. The view from the front of Mt. Vernon toward the river to the east was superb. It was essential that visitors who arrived via the river have an uninterrupted view of the manor house. It could not be marred by plantation buildings no matter how important they were. Washington's ice house was the only exception, but it was logically tucked below the lawn area, out of sight. At the same time, as the approach to the mansion by road was necessarily to the back of the building, it too needed an elegant treatment. Therefore Washington did not have the luxury of making his front yard the center of attention while relegating his work area to the back, as is common today.

The plan he eventually hit upon evolved, as do almost all good plans, gradually. When dealing with property of any scale, there is no substitute for living with one's land over a period of years to determine the best method of proceeding with the landscaping. This is especially true for inexperienced gardeners and designers as Washington certainly was at the time of his marriage.

The mansion, of course, had some planting around it before Washington returned from his military duties at the end of 1758. Whatever its original merit, as any Virginia gardener knows, without yearly attention most plant material can rather quickly get out of hand unless it is very carefully chosen. For all intents and purposes the grounds and the plantation fields had been largely abandoned years before the new owner took charge. It is hardly surprising, then, that Washington started over from scratch, especially because he was set upon enlarging his house. He also wanted outbuildings that reflected his projected needs.

The primary order of business was the establishment of a rectangular kitchen garden in 1760. The first of an eventual pair, this was located to the south, a lower garden, ideal for his fruit trees and to hasten the growth of his vegetables. As the area was fairly extensive and sloped besides, Washington laid out two terraces, one above the other, the lowest one containing his cold frames. Suitable paths of brick and turf gave access to the garden's various compartments. The whole was enclosed by a brick wall topped by a wooden picket fence, essential in a day before barbed wire secured livestock. The wall served important secondary functions. It provided protection from the wind and helped hold the heat of early spring days. Against its north side, which caught the sun, Washington could espalier his fruit trees. This training form, little known now, was favored both in England and by colonists like Washington who took their inspiration in such matters from abroad; once established, the trees are easier to care for and produce better fruit than do the free-standing sort. Fruit trees at Mt. Vernon were also espaliered on cordons to form hedges. These cordons were later replaced by boxwood, probably in 1798. Boxwood for hedges and for other edgings along the borders of the gardens and the parterres in front of the greenhouse were grown in his nursery.

As some rural Virginia gardeners still do, Washington then established an upper garden to the north. Vegetables were grown there, but flowers, trees, and plants of foreign origin overshadowed them. Experimentation was the rule for this gardener. His orangery, finished in 1789, added to the possibilities of what he could grow.

As for landscaping, Washington's initial efforts were concentrated on establishing a grove of trees at each end of his house to screen the mansion from work areas. While he had formulated the plans prior to the Revolutionary War, the trees were not planted until after he began soldiering. He wrote detailed instructions to his plantation manager in August 1776 from New York. The North Grove, said Washington, was to be composed of locust, the South Grove with "all the clever kind of Trees (especially flowering ones) . . . these to be interspersed here and there with ever greens. . . . [T]o these may be added the Wild flowering Shrubs of the larger kind."[4] Later, similar additions were made to the North Grove, and walks were added to both. The groves were deliberately overplanted, for as Washington was well aware it is easy to remove unwanted trees from any spot but only time, as he observed, can bring them to maturity.

After he had established the location of these basic features, he could proceed with further improvements after the conclusion of the war. To provide a suitable setting for the back of his house he established a bowling green, a feature of other great estates acknowledging the popular game. At its terminus was a view of the far woods beyond the white gate that opened to the lawn. The first order of business was to prepare the area for roads and plantings. For this he brought in field hands from the other farms which made up the Mt. Vernon plantation. In 1785 he laid out his serpentine carriage roads, to be shaded by a line of forest trees and screened from the gardens by dense plantings of flowering trees, shrubs, and small evergreens. By the following year the west wall of each garden was removed, and new ones curving to a point were installed. This change enlarged Washington's garden space and brought the gardens into better proportion with the new serpentine drives.

By the spring of 1788 grading to the west end of the bowling green had been completed. Grassy mounds, each dominated by a weeping willow, flanked the gate to the new entrance. Washington's so-called wilderness areas then received attention. Splayed extensions of the shrubberies, they were planted with tall-growing pines and bordered by hollies. Gravel walks were eventually made through them.

In the earlier years to establish his plantings Washington relied heaviliy on local native forest trees and shrubs that he himself scouted out on his own property, although he included old colonial favorites such as lilacs as well. In 1792 another large planting effort was under way, this time utilizing material from the William Bartram nursery in Philadelphia.

To the east of the house another large lawn area allowed an uninterrupted view of the Potomac. Shrubs were planted below the bluff, and trees were sited to frame the magnificent view. One of Washington's last activities before his death was to spend part of a day marking trees that he thought should be removed to open the view.

Our first president left another legacy to Americans in addition to Mt. Vernon: the city that bears his name. Without him it is doubtful the project would have been completed as it was. Only he could command the respect of all contending parties to get the job done. Once the politics of where in general to put the new capital had been worked out, Congress decided to ask George Washington to choose the exact site. The setting he chose was just upstream from his estate. Although there were houses in the vicinity, most notably in the village of Georgetown, the area consisted basically of thick forest. Abigail Adams aptly described the countryside as a "wild wilderness" dotted with clearings. The land to the south of the future White House and President's Park sloped to a marsh that bordered the river.

The site proposed for the presidential house had only an old cottage on it. This and the farm land around it had belonged to the Peerce family but was now in the hands of a speculator, Samuel Davidson, who sold part of this farm to the government. To complete the President's Park, David Burns sold part of his farm, which was adjacent to this plot. We can be sure that George Washington relied on all his experience at Mt. Vernon to create the proper setting for the executive mansion.

The project of building the new federal city was begun in 1791 with negotiations for the land the president had selected. He attached such importance to the matter that he himself led the government's delegation. He was also responsible for choosing Pierre Charles L'Enfant (with no salary or title) to design the new city, including the building that would house future presidents.

Washington was no stranger to architecture, of course, having made and executed many plans for Mt. Vernon over the years. The subject of the design for the President's House must have been much in his thoughts, but he was more concerned that it be large enough. The official residence in Philadelphia, the previous capital, had proven much too small. Weighing more heavily on his mind was the necessity of beginning construction of the quarters for the president and Congress as soon as possible, for he wanted the new capital to be firmly established on the Potomac before he left office.

Washington had good cause to worry. While L'Enfant was

Aquatint of Washington by George Isham Parkyns, 1794. (Library of Congress)

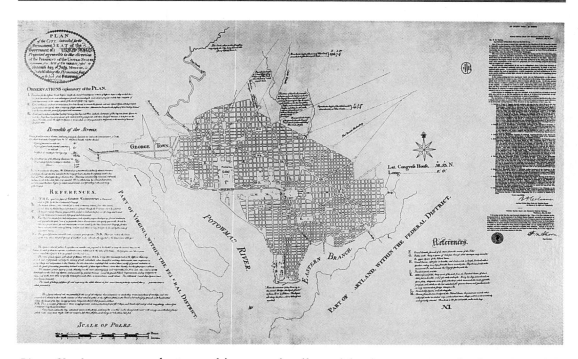

Pierre Charles L'Enfant's plan for the nation's capital. (National Archives)

busy working out details and having streets staked out, trouble was brewing. The Frenchman could get along with no one besides the president himself, both Philadelphians and New Yorkers were still trying to get the new capital in their respective cities, and L'Enfant's envisioned palatial President's House was regarded as an extravagance unsuited to the ideals of the new republic. The result of all the contention was the dismissal of L'Enfant, a design competition for the residence, and finally, the choice of James Hoban's entry as the competition's winner. With some modifications (the first by Washington himself, who increased the length and breadth by one-fifth and added some ornamentation to the plain façade), the resulting building became the structure we know today.

Even with Washington's alterations the White House is considerably smaller than the original palatial plans called for. The president personally set the center of the revised building to the north of the spot L'Enfant had chosen but used L'Enfant's line for the north wall. The front door at least would be where the Frenchman had drawn it. The cornerstone was laid on October 13, 1792.

The building's size, shape, and location as established by Washington would present problems to those in the future who would attempt to landscape it. Thus, although he died before the mansion was completed, Washington in effect determined much of what could and could not be done with planting trees, shrubs, and gardens and adding all the appurtenances that go with them. L'Enfant's palace, for all its pretensions, not only was of proper proportions for its site, but its location in his plan also provided one terminus of the axis of Pennsylvania Avenue with the Capitol at the other end. The first problem was eventually overcome by adding wings to the building, but the second prompted less adequate solutions. There is no evidence that Washington worried about either point, but he surely understood the consequences.

The earliest changes to the site were made by slaves hired from their masters. Soon skilled workmen were brought in. All needed lodging, so numerous small cottages were constructed on what would become the President's Park. One of these was owned by the architect James Hoban, who designed and built not only the first White House but also the second after the British burned the city in 1814. Hoban's cottage was rented by one Betsy Donahue, wife of a carpenter working on the mansion. She is remembered for opening a brothel in her quarters, a situation not looked upon favorably by the three-man commission the president had appointed to oversee development of the federal city. She was duly fined, and the house was torn down.

By the time John and Abigail Adams were expected to move in, the White House inside and out hardly presented a finished appearance. Much work remained to be done, but the Adamses did have the honor of being the first residents of a house that soon became known by people throughout the world.

John Adams
1797-1801

That John and Abigail Adams made only one contribution to the White House grounds was due to a lack of time, not interest. John Adams was determined from his earliest years to be a cultivator of the soil. The intention lasted a lifetime. He would insist to anyone who would listen that he was primarily a farmer. In his autobiography he refers to "the Amusements of Agriculture always delightefull to me."[1] He was always conscious of its importance irrespective of personal preferences. At age twenty-eight he described agriculture as "the Nursing Mother of every Art, Science, Trade and Profession in civilized society."[2]

As a fourteen-year-old, the boy did not share his father's desire that his first-born child go to college. John's teachers until then had failed to challenge this brilliant youngster who could tell his father with great certitude that he did not love books. He was interested in the outdoors, in sports, but reading? He wanted nothing more than to become a husbandman working his own fields.

His father put his son to a test: Spend the whole of a farmer's day with him at work instead of interspersing farm chores with school, roaming the family property, hunting, dreaming, and other pursuits of youth. After dinner on the test day John Sr. asked the youngster whether he was satisfied with his choice. Although the work had been very hard and very muddy (as John Jr. recalled many years later), he had answered, "Yes, sir, I like it very well."[3] His father, though, had long had other ideas for his namesake. He told young John that *he* didn't like the decision and that the boy *would* go to school. After a change in teachers, within the year John Adams the second discovered the joys of books, which led him in imagination far beyond his home in Braintree, Massachusetts.

At age fifteen he entered Harvard. Eight years later—after graduation, a stint as a teacher in Worcester, and an apprenticeship in law—Adams returned to Braintree. In another dozen years his experiences as a lawyer, under the circumstances of the time, inevitably led him into politics. While he might go through the motions of claiming it his duty, politics in time became more than that to him despite periods of profound discouragement. In reality he thrived on it despite his protestations to the contrary. Nevertheless the wellspring of his content, in addition to his wife and family, was always his farm. It was his rock, the center of his existence; and its concerns, in addition to providing a much-needed income, were always on his mind.

A Massachusetts farm in those days was very different from the plantations George Washington knew. There was a considerable difference in the number of acres held, and the labor was by free men, not slaves. While a farm like the Adamses' could provide little more than life's basic necessities, few New England farmers willingly went into debt for life's luxuries. Tight management was therefore essential.

In other respects, once tobacco had ceased to dominate Virginia fields, the two states had much in common. And a farmer who loved his land was surely the same in both regions. Wherever Adams went, at home or abroad, he observed the farms of others, noted their attributes, and compared these with his own property. He swapped information with any knowledgeable person along the way. Whenever he was gone from home he fretted about what he had left behind. On a trip to springs in Connecticut in hopes of restoring his health, he lamented, "I want to see my Wife, my Children, my Farm, my Horse, Oxen, Cows, Walls, Fences, Workmen, Office, Books and Clerks."[4]

When he had time to sort out his thoughts, his introspective musings led him to conclusions such as the following, which appeared in a January 1759 entry in his diary: "But I'le not forego the Pleasure of ranging the Woods, Climbing Cliffs, walking in fields, Meadows, by Rivers, Lakes, &c., and confine my self to Chamber for nothing. I'le have some Boon, in Return, Exchange, fame, fortune, or something."[5] The twenty-four-year-old made good on his promise to himself.

Being torn away from his beloved fields and the world of nature was always wrenching despite the fame, if not fortune, he would soon earn. His first entry in his new diary, dated November 18, 1755, had consisted in its totality of a description of the great earthquake of that date. The natural world around him is mentioned again and again in its pages. He condensed his sentiment on the subject to one sentence in 1759: "Oh Nature! how [bright?]

and beautiful thou art."[6] Its hold on him extended to vignettes that barely would have registered with others, such as an entry from 1770. Adams had gone to visit a friend overnight. The next morning he went to see how his horse had fared. He wrote, "My little mare had provided for herself by leaping out of a bare Pasture into a neighboring Lott of mowing ground, and had filled herself, with Grass and Water. These are important Materials for History no doubt. My Biographer will scarcely introduce my little Mare, and her Adventures in quest of Feed and Water."[7] There you are, Mr. Adams.

James Madison summed it up in 1822 in these words: "It is among the proofs of Mr. Adams's comprehensive patriotism that he called the attention of his Country at so early a day, and in so impressive a mode, to the subject of Natural History, then so little an object of American science. . . ."[8]

Adams's diary is filled with the proof. He noted, for example, that he found worms on "English Grass and Grain and Indian Corn." He reported seeing a captured young crow and was amazed at its ugliness, but he would give no quarter to its place in nature's scheme of things. He devoted considerable space in his diary to the subject of kelp, which had proved an excellent manure. On February 27, 1756, he recorded that Halley's comet was expected that year. The report was mistaken; the comet did not appear until 1759; however, Adams does not tell us if he saw it, despite numerous other entries for this period.

Astronomy, though, was out of the mainstream of Adams's greatest interests. Upon his return to Braintree from Worcester in the spring of 1759, Adams decided to make a *Common Place Book of Agriculture.* Considering his youth and the number of years he had been away from agricultural activities, the subjects he proposed to include in his book are remarkable in extent. They cover literally every environment, every plant and animal, every tool, every practice a farmer of his time and location could be expected to know about. Unrecognized by his father, the list shows that the son had at fourteen, despite his few years, been a very keen observer of life on the farm. Of interest to the modern home gardener is the lack of variety in the vegetables, although this is typical of the 1700s. These were potatoes, cabbages, peas, and beans of different sorts, "Colly flower and sellery," turnips, parsnips, horseradish, and various herbs. "Dandelyons" were included for the garden as a source of greens, and Adams did not forget flowers, listing only pinks, tulips, roses, and white and red peonies but adding "&c."

It was fortunate that he had such matters firmly in mind even though he did not elaborate on any of his proposed entries and there is no indication that the project was ever consummated. Two years later his father was dead. His property was divided with a third going to his wife and two-thirds to his sons. As John had received a college education, he was given less valuable acreage than his brothers. Nonetheless this bequest was still substantial for a Massachusetts farmer. It included the house adjacent to John's birthplace and a barn as well as ten acres adjoining it plus thirty acres of woods, pasture, and orchard in other locations in town. Adams's brother Peter Boylston received the more valuable homestead, and his youngest brother, Elihu, a farm in Randolph a few miles to the south. By 1764 John was married, and this added pressure to his need to be a successful farmer.

Abigail Adams was a truly unusual woman for her time, with talents and interests that went far beyond those of almost all of her contemporaries. In every respect she was an excellent match for John in his dual life as farmer and politician. While Adams virtually dictated his wife's responsibilities in regard to their farm and the education of their children, we can be sure she would have coped well—and indeed did—without his direction. Adams, despite his sometimes blustering manner, was duly appreciative of his wife's efforts and abilities and considered her his equal. He wrote her in April 1794, "My dearest friend [his usual salutation], The post of the day brought me your kind letter of 26th ultimo. The more I am charmed with your bravery and activity in farming, the more I am mortified that my letters in answer to yours are so insignificant and insipid. I must leave all your agriculture to your judgement and the advice of your assistants. . . . You are so valorous and noble a farmer that I feel little anxious about agriculture. Manure in hills if you think best, but manure your barley ground and harrow it well."[9]

Because of John's many absences from home, it can truthfully be said that the Adamses' family and gardening were a joint affair, a partnership. Their very lives depended on both their efforts. Theirs was a true family farm. When John was away, Abigail took charge. The orders were hers, as was the task of hiring and firing workers. She paid the men and women in her employ after directing them at their various jobs. In short, she was the embodiment of the pre-Revolutionary woman who was expected to actively shoulder the burdens of running the life of her family and community. (It was not until after the war that the cloistering of women of her social background began.)

One of John's major concerns was to add to his holdings. This seems to have been an emotional need rather than a totally rational one for a man who had no family fortune to tap and whose career as a lawyer was frequently interrupted by political offices—none of which ever added significantly to his bank account.

In 1774, though he was aware of the obstacles, he purchased the Adams homestead from his brother for £440. This consisted of the Adams house in which he had been born thirty-nine years before, a barn with thirty-five acres, and eighteen acres of pasture, well walled in, on the north common of town. The price must have been, in truth, beyond his means. On the other hand, ownership by some other family would have been unthinkable, although the pasture could have conceivably been let go. Adams justified the purchase on the basis of the numerous red cedars he acquired; he thought that with good pruning each would in twenty years be worth a shilling. Meanwhile his cows could browse the greens, and he could use the bare branches for fuel.

He noted in his diary, "This is a fine addition, to what I had there before, of arable, and Meadow. The Buildings and the Water, I wanted very much. That beautifull, winding, meandering Brook, which runs thro this farm, always delighted me. How shall I improve it? Shall I try to introduce fowl Meadow And Herds Grass, into the Meadows? or still better Cover and Herdsgrass? I must ramble over it, and take a View. The Meadow is a great Object."[10]

In 1776 Adams bought from the widow of his youngest brother, Elihu, twenty-eight acres of woods for forty shillings per acre. In 1787 he asked Dr. Cotton Tufts to buy "That Piece of land [Tufts had told Abigail about] and every other, that adjoins upon me." Adams explained, "My view is to lay fast hold of the Town of Braintree and embrace it, with both my arms and all my might. There to live—there to die—there to lay my bones—and there to plant one of my sons, in the Profession of the Law and the practice of Agriculture, like his father.—To this end, I wish to purchase as much land there, as my utmost forces will allow that I may have farm enough to amuse me and employ me, as long as I live."[11] Tufts, the husband of Abigail's aunt and a longtime friend to the couple, had just negotiated the purchase of a large, handsome house in Braintree, less than three miles from the house in which John was born, with eighty-three acres of fields, pastures, woodland, and salt marsh.

Abigail aided and abetted her husband's acquisitive nature. While John was abroad she bought a seven-acre parcel that had belonged to John's uncle, paying $200 for it. She decided it held 45 cords of wood and was well worth the money asked. John referred to it as "that fine Grove which I have loved and admired from my cradle."[12] Other land purchases were also made, all small, as befitted the Massachusetts coast. Abigail mused that her husband "thinks he never saved any thing but what he vested in land."[13] However, by 1803, with the failure of his London bankers, John was forced to begin selling some of his land. His son John Quincy bought the family homestead at this time.

New Englanders had learned after a hundred years and more that their land was most useful for raising cattle. The thin, stony soil quickly wore away unless it was covered with English grasses. Even with these, soil fertility was always a problem. Yet men would live in this corner of the continent. Adam's pride was his dairy herd, the rationale for all his composting, buying, and clearing new pastures and constructing the fences to keep his cows safe and a solid barn to carry them over the harsh winter months. His hard work and his attention to detail paid off. His acres produced as much as they were capable of.

Naturally, improvements had to be made to his farm. This entry in his diary for October 24, 1762, reveals very well what was going through his mind on this subject. How much of this work he did himself is questionable, considering his schedule as a lawyer, yet when he did get out into his fields it was always with gusto. The entry is long, but it provides a good picture of life on a Massachusetts farm.

My Thoughts are running continually from the orchard to the Pasture and from thence to the swamp, and thence to the House and Barn and Land adjoining. Sometimes I am at the orchard Ploughing up Acre after Acre and Planting, pruning Apple Trees, mending Fences, carting Dung. Sometimes in the Pasture, digging stones, clearing Bushes, Pruning Trees, building Wall to redeem Posts and Rails, and sometimes removing Button Trees down to my house. Sometimes I am at the old swamp, burning Bushes, digging stumps and Roots, cutting Ditches, across the Meadow, and against my Uncle, and am sometimes at the other End of the Town, buying Posts and Rails, to Fence against my Uncle and against the Brook, and am sometimes Ploughing the Upland, with 6 Yoke of oxen, and planting Corn, Potatoes, &c. and digging up the Meadow and sowing onions, planting cabbages &c. &c.

Sometimes I am at the Homestead running Cross Fences, and planting Potatoes by the Acre, and Corn by the two Acres, and running a Ditch along the Line between me and Field, and a Fence along the Brook [against] my Brother and another Ditch in the Middle from Fields Line to the Meadow. Sometimes am Carting Gravel from the Neighboring Hills, and sometimes Dust from the streets upon the fresh Meadow. And sometimes plowing, sometimes digging those Meadows, to introduce Clover and other English Grasses.[14]

The following year Adams was urging in an essay in the *Boston Gazette* improvements in agriculture by persons "who have any Advantage of Leisure, Education, or Fortune to amuse themselves, at convenient opportunities, with the study, and the Practice too, of Husbandry." He exhorted such individuals by telling them, "In making Experiments, upon the Varieties of soils, and Manures, Grains and Grasses, Trees, and Bushes, and in your Enquiries into the Course and operation of Nature in the Production of these, you will find as much Employment for your Ingenuity, and as high a Gratification to a good Taste, as in any Business or amusement you can chuse to pursue."[15]

In February 1771 Adams himself was involved with a committee of the Massachusetts House of Representatives to consider a plan for a society to encourage the arts, agriculture, manufactures, and commerce within the colony. He followed up on this in early 1776 by writing three of four resolutions for encouraging agriculture and manufacturing that the Continental Congress approved in March of that year. Each colony was urged to form a society to promote this goal.

Of more interest to today's gardener is Adams's recipe for manure:

Take the Soil and Mud, which you cutt up and throw out when you dig Ditches in a Salt Marsh, and put 20 Load of it in a heap. Then take 20 Loads of common Soil or mould of Upland and Add to the other. Then to the whole add 20 Loads of Dung, and lay the whole in a Heap, and let it lay 3 months, then take your Spades And begin at one End of the Heap, and dig it up and throw it into another Heap, there let it lie, till the Winter when the Ground is frozen, and then cart it on, to your English Grass Land.—Ten or 20 Loads to an Acre, as you choose.—Rob. Temple learnt it in England,

and first practised it at Ten Hills. From him the Gentry at Cambridge have learnt it, and they all Practice it.[16]

The diary, a sure commentary on what Adams was involved with, was, as he admitted, not faithfully kept. As regards his farm, he regains his pen again briefly in 1795. He discusses lime and an acquaintance's methods with crops. It is not until the following summer, when he recognized that he might well become the next president of the United States, that he bore down hard on farm projects. He records information about his corn, his barley, potatoes, English hay, and clover, but his greatest pleasure was derived from his new barn near the site of an old one that had been taken down by his father when the latter had built a new one. John was immersed in planning his own new barn—a structure forty-five feet long and proportionately wide. He must also have found special satisfaction in harvesting many of the red cedars that he had thought justified the expense of buying his brother's pasture on the north common. The cedars were not sold; instead, they became part of the barn then under construction, and this probably pleased him more than the cash he might have received. The thinning achieved another desired result: "We have opened the Prospect so that the Meadows and Western Mountain may be distinctly seen."[17]

Time, however, worked against him in another spot. "My beautiful Grove, so long preserved by my Father and my Uncle, proves to be all rotten," he wrote. "More than half the Trees We cutt are so defective as to be unfit for any Use but the fire. I shall save the White Oaks, and cutt the rest." Another cause for concern was an ancient apple tree "with Apples enough upon it to make two Barrells of Cyder" that was sacrificed to the "Beauty and Convenience of the Road."[18] The selectmen of Quincy had decreed the road be straightened and widened.

To care for his farm Adams hired both black and white men. Domestic staff and even his widowed mother's new husband were pressed into service when necessary. The number employed depended on the season, with the summer months requiring the most. In the summer of 1796 he mentions by name more than a dozen workers plus his coachman and Briesler, his longtime house man. The part-time help was employed for a set number of months or for a particular job, such as haying. Those who were not tenants were mostly from the neighborhood. Performance of job duties sometimes left something to be desired in the eyes of this hard-working couple. Drinking was often at the basis of poor workmanship, and of course the work was heavy and probably uninspiring to men and boys who had no roots on this land.

For her part Abigail was not afraid to personally tackle harvesting the corn if need be but feared she would "make a poor figure at digging potatoes."[19] She tarred the trunks of the apple trees, just as John himself did when he was there, for six weeks to prevent the tent caterpillar from doing damage. Her normal duties at home (which she thoroughly enjoyed) were skimming her milk (at five o'clock in the morning, she reported); making butter and cheese; tending her turkeys, geese, and chickens; and working in her garden. Supervisory duties filled her days according to the season. Fall was particularly busy. Apple cider had to be made properly and stored (fifty barrels brought satisfaction to the Adamses), and the apples and pears that could be eaten fresh had to be continually picked over so that one rotten one did not spoil its neighbors. Apples also had to be dried for pies, potatoes and vegetables had to be stored, and jellies had to be put up. A supply of meat was also required. Abigail Adams, one of the most intellectual women of her era, was also a practicing farmer's wife and reveled in it.

When John went abroad and when she later followed, it was she who arranged for the travelers' needs. On John's first trip with their son John Quincy, food supplies included six chickens to provide eggs and ultimately fresh meat, two fat sheep, a barrel of apples, five bushels of corn, sugar, tea, chocolate, and assorted additional items. When she herself crossed the ocean her little party included a cow to furnish fresh milk, cream, and butter.

To accomplish all this, life in Braintree was devoted to doing things properly. Just as John would never think of cheating his fields, so thin and rocky, of their yearly application of compost, or of denying his dairy herd the best feed and housing he could provide, neither would Abigail waste food the farm produced or neglect to instruct her household helpers in the most efficient and best manner of accomplishing necessary tasks to make the farm operate smoothly.

In this busy life there was little time for flowers, although both husband and wife were appreciative of their beauty. John found relaxation picking bugs off his wife's roses. Abigail wrote "the beauties which my garden unfolds to my view from the window at which I write tempt me to forget the past and rejoice in the full bloom of the pear, the apple, the plum, the peach, and the rich luxuriance of the grass plats, interspersed with the cowslip, the daffy, and the columbine, all unite to awaken the most pleasing sensations."[20]

Efforts toward landscaping must have been minimal. John does not seem to have been interested in this phase of gardening. His tour of English gardens with Thomas Jefferson illustrates this, although both clutched their respective volumes of Thomas Whately's *Observations on Modern Gardening* to give them good guidance as to each estate's prominent features. At one stop Jefferson discovered that Whately had failed to include a Palladian bridge in his description. John Adams very possibly did not know—or care—what a Palladian bridge was. He was touring the gardens for a different reason. As always in his life, he was thrilled with the general aspects that nature presented. But while he found beauty abroad, one gets the impression he felt that the vistas around Braintree could not be surpassed.

Adams was basically a down-to-earth man, finding his happiness in what was given him at home. He named his farm Montezillo. He explained to a friend, "Mr. Jefferson lives at Monticello the lofty Mountain. I live at *Montezillo* a little Hill."[21] In truth he did not think to christen his place until 1814, years after he had moved to his new, larger house. He had indeed thought of several names before hitting upon Montezillo. Unlike Jefferson, he used the name infrequently. He was, after all, an unpretentious man, a New England farmer.

Before he and Abigail moved to the yet unfinished White House in the new capital city of Washington, Adams demanded only one thing be accomplished by the time they arrived in the fall of 1800: He must have a vegetable garden to supply food for the coming winter. Landscaping was left to his friend and successor, Thomas Jefferson.

Thomas Jefferson
1 8 0 1 - 9

Although Thomas Jefferson is a president well known for his gardening interests, he has never been given the recognition in this field that he truly deserves. As with Washington and Adams before him, Jefferson's occupation was farming. After all, virtually everyone in those days, except for the comparative few who lived in the larger towns like Philadelphia and New York, tilled the soil, although a rural man's day might also be spent as a lawyer, doctor, politician, merchant, or preacher. Jefferson was trained in the law. As a tobacco planter he could in good conscience leave his fields to the care of overseers with minimal supervision on his part. However, like Washington, he was caught in the decline of his soils along with a decline in the English market for the leaf, so he too made the conversion to being a wheat farmer.

Despite his background in the legal profession, Jefferson was making a statement when he built his mansion on top of his little mountain. Although his law practice was centered in more populated areas of the colony of Virginia, he was to be a man of the country. His father, Peter, had been one of the early settlers of Albemarle County. By 1743, though, at Thomas's birth, the hard edges of the forest had been worn off. By the time of his marriage in 1771, his bride, the widow Martha Wayles Skelton, whose home was The Forest in Charles City near Williamsburg, would not have felt too daring living within sight of the growing village of Charlottesville, even though it was far inland.

Jefferson's youth, like that of other country boys, was spent roaming the family property. In his case, his oldest and much-loved sister, Jane, accompanied him on his rambles, the two botanizing as they went. These forays made an indelible impression on him and pointed him irreversibly into the life of a farmer, gardener, landscaper, and naturalist. He repeated again and again throughout his life that, next to his family and books, the outdoors was most important to him.

While he took great pride in Monticello and in his second home, Poplar Forest in Bedford County, Virginia, Jefferson's correspondence and other personal records have little to do with these or his other building ventures in terms of their architecture. Architecture did not command the lyricism so evident in his statements regarding growing plants. Jefferson enjoyed tinkering and creating, the basis of his house building as well as making things at his forge, but architecture was an avocation. While he hoped with his building to set a good example to his fellow Americans, he understood very clearly that agriculture was the foundation of any nation. His forays into classical and contemporary literature provided him with plenty of examples to show that a nation's rise and fall hinged directly and totally on how its inhabitants treated their soil, their water supply, their forests. After his initial flurry of being a lawyer, except when pressured into politics, Jefferson deliberately devoted his days and his energy into his vocation: that of farmer. (His references to his political offices are always invaded by the often written, sometimes implied question "Why must it be me?")

Jefferson's philosophy of land was simple. He said, "For of all things it is that of which I am most tenacious." His land holdings were based primarily in Albemarle County. Some of them, including the tract he named Monticello, he inherited from his father. They totaled over 5,200 acres. He bought other land himself. After his marriage and upon the death of his father-in-law, John Wayles, in 1773 he also acquired some 4,800 acres, known as Poplar Forest, in Bedford County, and other smaller properties elsewhere. Some of these possessions he was to sell over the years, but the heart of the Poplar Forest tract assumed increasing importance to him because the tobacco it produced was significant in quantity and good in quality. It became the means by which he could make payments on his debts. His major obligation was to English creditors of his father-in-law, who had left at his death one of the colony's greatest debts along with extensive land holdings and slaves. Jefferson's share of the debt came to over £4,000, an enormous sum. Wayles, like so many of his social peers (and Jefferson himself), had lived high on tobacco, always expecting next year's yield of this glorious crop to balance the books. Meanwhile, additional costly goods were ordered to embellish the persons and homes of the planter. Of course, this was gambling, and Jefferson was to pay a heavy price for Wayles's errors of judgment—as well as his own—in this regard.

Jefferson's conversion from tobacco planter to wheat farmer

came in 1794. By then he had served in a variety of public positions, including six years abroad and most recently as George Washington's secretary of state. He felt he had earned the right of retirement despite Washington's request that he remain at his post. During all these years he had had little time to really observe his farm firsthand and reflect on what he saw. When he took a close look he was appalled to see how his house and his fields had suffered from his absence. His wife's death in 1782 had left him both shaken in spirit and with two young daughters whose futures totally depended on him. By 1793 with Martha, his oldest, married and Maria approaching young womanhood he could see more clearly his path to the future.

Up to this point Jefferson had exhibited a curious detachment regarding critical farm operations at Monticello. To some degree this attitude would continue there and at Poplar Forest until his death. All through his life he was never demanding of his employees or slaves, always ready where possible to excuse their failings. His control of expenditures was equally lax, and he could easily be accused of being penny wise and pound foolish. In other words, in these basics he could be faulted as a less than efficient manager of his plantations. In all other areas, however, he radiated light like the brightest star in the darkness of space.

Following Washington's lead, Jefferson in 1793 laid out a plan of crop rotations for his fields for the upcoming years. His rotation plan, later modified, consisted of five years of crops followed by three years of clover. Typically, he consulted others whose opinion he valued, including James Madison and his own new son-in-law, Thomas Mann Randolph.

Jefferson's father had planted wheat only for family use; his son would go into large-scale production. As for tobacco, Thomas was unable to stop growing it at Monticello. It was a certain way to bring in much-needed cash to supplement the money he got from his wheat and from Bedford tobacco (and later Bedford wheat as well). Corn had been a staple crop from the earliest days of the colony. Although Jefferson was aware of its abuse to the soil, he was equally aware that his slaves and his livestock depended on it for food. He could only hope that the years of clover would undo the damage corn and even wheat did to his land. (Tobacco was confined each year to newly cleared plots or those cleared the previous year; the land was then used for other crops or left to go back into brush and trees.)

Especially now that he was a wheat farmer, Jefferson's farming operations required a great deal more of his time, and new tools as well. For one thing, he was in need of a better plow. Fortunately while he was abroad from 1785 to 1789 he could observe what English and other European farmers used. He quickly concluded that their plows were inefficient primarily because of their moldboards or lack of moldboards altogether. (The moldboard is the curved plate of a plow that turns over the furrow slice.) His tinker's mind came up with the reason for the poor performance as well as a solution.

When he returned home he made a model of a replacement, then asked the judgment of his son-in-law and friends in the science community to validate his claim that his design of a moldboard produced the least resistance to the plow as it was pulled through the soil. Later he had a full-size implement constructed. His "moldboard of least resistance" brought him a gold medal from the Society of Agriculture of Paris and the honor of being named one of its foreign associates. The Board of Agriculture of England received a model of the original as well as a model incorporating Jefferson's improvements. At home, local farmers received the invention with much less enthusiasm, new ideas being usually avoided down on the ordinary farm.

Jefferson's tinkering extended to other farm implements. Whatever he came up with was never patented, always freely given for others to use. He believed, as did Washington and Adams, that it was up to those who were better off financially to make experiments. The poor dirt farmer could not afford to fail.

Jefferson's gardens and orchards devoted to human food came in for their share of experimentation. His choice of what to grow was aided and abetted by other gardeners, who felt sure that Jefferson would also want *their* favorites. These varieties he usually managed to tuck in somewhere among the rest. Only one man was able to overwhelm completely the Jefferson garden: André Thoüin, whom Jefferson had become acquainted with in France. Every year transportation could be arranged across the ocean Thoüin sent packets of seeds of choice plants that came to him in his capacity as director of the French National Garden. These packets Jefferson was forced to direct to others who had the time and expertise to grow them and evaluate the results of their growth under American conditions. (In 1808, for example, Thoüin sent seeds of 700 different plants.)

Jefferson himself was largely a vegetarian. In addition, he needed sizable quantities of fruits and vegetables for the large number of family members and guests who inhabited or visited Monticello. He coped by establishing two major orchards and an enormous vegetable garden. The orchard on the north side of his mountain was devoted at first to cider apples. Later peach trees were interplanted. He had put his first fruit trees on the south side of the mountain in 1769. He recognized that this slope held the most favorable growing conditions, and his main efforts were directed there. Before he was finished, his workmen had cleared tons of dirt to form a series of three flat platforms totaling 80 feet wide and 1,000 feet long on which to plant vegetables and a few fruits. To hold back the dirt on the slope, boulders weighing up to a half ton each were set without mortar to form a massive wall up to 12 feet high. Below the wall he put his fruit trees, his vineyard, and, against the wall, assorted crops that in spring and fall would benefit from the trapped solar heat.

With such an enormous expanse of garden it was imperative that Jefferson divide the space into smaller units, both for ease in taking care of the plants and for keeping track of what was where. Numbered squares, rows, and sticks were then translated into his *Garden Book* for easy planning and reference. He was certainly a record keeper and experimenter par excellence. Jefferson was very serious about his garden. His slave Isaac remembered his master this way, "For amusement he would work sometimes in the garden for half an hour at a time in right good earnest in the cool of the evening."[1] Without doubt Jefferson devoutly wished he could do so more often.

Because of his detailed records we today have a standard against which to judge the fruits and vegetables of his day. The strawberries were minute: 100 were required to fill a half pint. So were his peas tiny. One variety required 2,000 to fill a pint; another, 2,500. His cucumbers were small, spiny, and dry-fleshed; his tomatoes, poor-tasting. Later plant breeders would work their miracles. Nevertheless, Jefferson still ate well. Unlike most people of his era he did not confine himself to the easy-to-grow cabbages, onions, turnips, and field corn. From earliest spring to late fall he took a succession of crops directly from his garden. Over the winter he tried to keep hardy leafy vegetables like kale alive, and his storage areas were filled with produce from his plots.

The same held true for fruits. Every kind that came his way was tried. This does not mean that he was necessarily successful. For example, despite innumerable stones planted and germinated, despite grafted cuttings, Monticello's weather was too variable to allow for the successful growing of peaches; periodic frosts killed every standing tree. Apples did much better. These were supplemented with pears, apricots, plums, and cherries. He grew a full variety of nuts too. In the early years he grafted some of his trees. Later he depended on workmen to do this job. Still later, Jefferson bought grafted stock when it became available from nurseries. Despite his records, exactly what he had in his orchards is difficult to determine. Included in his collection were the melon peach and sugar pear. Others were described by color or from whom Jefferson had received them. In reconstructing the gardens and orchards, Peter Hatch, superintendent of grounds at Monticello, was occasionally hard pressed to figure out what the names meant, let alone find the same varieties for replacements.

Jefferson's enthusiasm for horticulture extended to his establishing a vegetable garden and orchard at Poplar Forest, albeit on a scale much-reduced from that of his gardens and orchards at Monticello. Given that he went to Bedford (ninety miles away) only three or four times a year after he began building his home there in 1806, and his visits were of comparatively short duration, his determination is commendable. His neighbors there often brought in food upon his arrival, which helped.

Food plants were, of course, essential, but Jefferson lived for more. He must have trees. He had, after all, by necessity cleared off the top of his little mountain at Monticello in order to build his house. The area around it must therefore be landscaped and vistas created. He made his first plan just before his marriage January 1, 1772. Strangely, two-thirds of this lengthy landscaping dissertation dealt with death, not life. His beloved sister Jane, who had died six years before, was still much on his mind. But he concluded on a more cheerful note, listing the tasks common to owners of uncleared property, such as cutting out stumps and undergrowth. He also jotted down the names of trees and shrubs that might occupy the site.

He got started putting in stock in 1778 when he planted calycanthus, Magnolia tripetala, aspens, and Chinaberry trees. Then there was a lapse due to the Revolutionary War, his wife's precarious health and ultimate death, and his later service abroad. Although he bought a large number of trees in 1791 in anticipation of his retirement, landscaping of Monticello did not proceed in earnest until after he left the presidency in 1809.

As president, Jefferson had on a daily basis landscaping problems right before his eyes. Extravagant with his money when it came to embellishing Monticello and Poplar Forest, he was a model of frugality when it came to public expenditures. Yet something had to be done to the grounds of the new White House and the avenue that linked it with the Capitol. His first order of business was to remove the outhouse that stood outside his door and install two water closets upstairs in the house itself. Some of the wooden sheds left over from construction were economically converted to houses for goats, sheep, and fowl. Cows made do with temporary shelter, the horses in something more substantial. As the animals found food where they could around the immediate grounds, it was difficult to establish order, especially when more important governmental matters demanded attention by the president.

Nevertheless, Congress understood its responsibility for planning the environment in which the new public buildings stood. During Jefferson's terms of office no outdoor task was more important than making Pennsylvania Avenue something more than a rutted frontier trail, providing for drives to the White House door and surrounding its grounds with a stone wall. In this the president had some help from an unexpected source: the Federalist William Plumer, who complained that the rough fence which originally surrounded the President's House was not fit for the yard of a barn.

These were just the bare necessities. Benjamin Latrobe, appointed surveyor of public buildings by Jefferson in 1803,

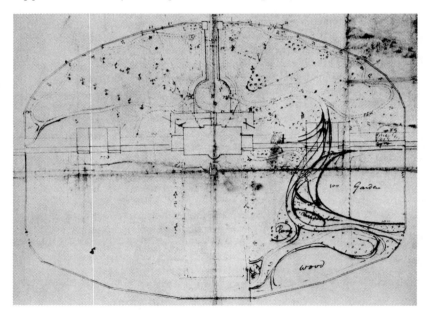

worked with him in devising a suitable landscaping plan for the large area surrounding the mansion. Major Pierre Charles L'Enfant, who had first been chosen for the job, had proven impossible to work with. The palace he had envisioned for the president's use was much too large for an American public more used to cottages, but its siting, upon which the location of the roads surrounding the palace were determined, caused permanent landscaping problems both front and back. In L'Enfant's plan roads arranged in sunlike rays came to a point at the front entrance. This idea was abandoned when the President's Park was extended to the north, which truncated the effect. President Jefferson did not like straight lines in his landscaping. Perhaps he considered this new arrangement the lesser of two evils. To the south the mansion no longer formed the terminus of the axis of Pennsylvania Avenue from the Capitol, but here was a solution more to his liking: the creation of a triple arch at the entrance to the grounds. (This was torn down during Andrew Johnson's term.) A graceful curving drive through a second arch immediately adjacent to the building provided access to the front courtyard. (Because the mortar was not allowed to set long enough, the arch collapsed. The ruins were not removed until 1819, during James Monroe's adminstration.)

For landscaping purposes, Jefferson and Latrobe divided the immediate White House grounds in two. The north section at the front of the mansion was designated for public use. The south grounds, which overlooked the Potomac River, were to be private despite the entrance at the southeast from Pennsylvania Avenue. Liberal use of trees created screens to soften the lines of the

house on all sides. To the southeast grounds Jefferson added a large garden area for both ornamental and edible plants, arranged in parterres. Although nothing came of it while he was in office, under the guidance of James Madison's steward it was planted. The site was retained as the White House flower garden until 1859, in James Buchanan's term. Planting of trees on the grounds while Jefferson was president seems to have been limited to two loads of aspen he sent for from Monticello at the end of his second term. Where they were put was not recorded.

Early in 1803 Jefferson saw to the planting of trees along Pennsylvania Avenue. Presented with several possible plans he chose one that featured a double row of Lombardy poplars on either side of the street. This tree, only recently introduced from Europe, had by then been extensively propagated both by indi-

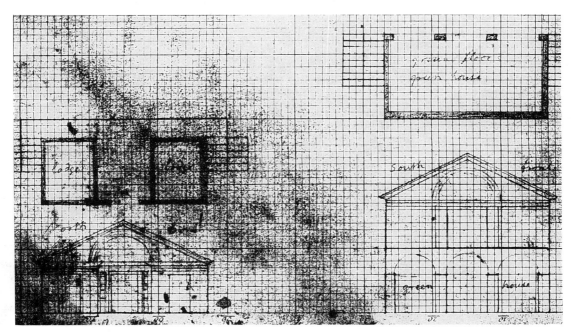

viduals and the Prince nursery if not other businesses. The trees were gotten from General Masons Island and Mt. Vernon, where George Washington had been making cuttings until his death. The cost? Twelve and a half cents each. However, the trees had to be boxed to prevent damage from wandering cattle and horses, and this brought the total expense to $1.00 per tree. Jefferson naturally envisioned the planting of additional trees of other varieties parallel to the fast-growing poplars, but money ran out before this could be accomplished while he was still in office.

As president, Jefferson also had the opportunity to set in motion the Lewis and Clark expedition (1804–6) to the Pacific northwest. In 1792 he had instigated a similar expedition, this one sponsored by the American Philosophical Society and led by the French botanist André Michaux, who was then studying plants

Early speculation that this T. J. drawing was for the Monticello vegetable garden was dashed when the building foundations there were discovered. More likely, this garden house was designed for the west wing of the White House, although it was never built for lack of funds. (Coolidge Collection, Massachusetts Historical Society)

45

in America. The mission was soon aborted when Michaux was recalled by his government. Meriwether Lewis, whom Jefferson had hired as his presidential secretary, more than made up for the earlier disappointment. Initial planning for the expedition was done in Jefferson's office at the White House, and the president followed the intrepid band in spirit every step of the way.

Although the ostensible reason for the journey was to determine the commercial possibilities of the newly acquired Louisiana territory, its real function was to acquire botanical and natural history information. Spoils of the expedition included many new species and even new genera of plants that Lewis, after his extensive training by Jefferson and other botanists, determined worthy of bringing back. The president reserved a few for himself, and most of the remainder were given to Bernard McMahon

to propagate. McMahon, a Philadelphia nurseryman, had been a major backer of the expedition and helped establish its goals. The two most important plants to come to the attention of easterners were the mahonia (Oregon grape holly), named for McMahon, and the osage orange, which soon provided fencing material for pioneer families on the prairies.

In November 1804 Jefferson was reelected president by a tremendous majority. He had been diligent, he had done his best, but a constant thought was that after four more years he would be a free man, finally able to do what he had longed to do for so many years: live at Monticello, leaving his home only when he so chose. His thoughts turned there ever more frequently.

The enlargement of his house was slowly but surely going forward. Knowing its precise dimensions, he could now plan his landscaping with more assurance. Once again he set down plans

In 1803 T. J. chose double rows of Lombardy poplars for Pennsylvania Avenue. (Library of Congress)

47

for the improvement of Monticello. These were of the same general, idealized nature as those he had written in 1771. Like the first set, many if not most of these ideas never came to fruition. Two years later he became more practical as the deadline of his return home approached: He drew in the locations of the different features of his mountaintop. By 1807 he had created two more plans. The first confined itself to landscaping the house foundation. He was at Monticello that spring, long enough to supervise the planting. A gravel walk was laid out, as was the Ellipse. In June he outlined to his oldest grandchild, Anne, his plan for the west lawn at the back of the house. This plan was dominated by the now-famous formal, generally oval-shaped, serpentine walk. He explained to Anne, his chief gardening assistant, that this would permit more room for the variety of flowers he had in mind. (He had included some flowers in the beds around the house foundation.) The walk and flower beds were set out in 1808.

Although flowers constitute his first entry in his *Garden Book*, as Jefferson explained to a French gardening friend in 1803, "I rarely ever planted a flower in my life. But when I return to live at Monticello . . . I believe I shall become a florist. The labours of the year, in that line, are repaid within the year, and death, which will be at my door, shall find me unembarrassed in long lived undertakings."[2] (Jefferson was unduly pessimistic; he lived until 1826.)

Jefferson's new-found interest in flowers was something he could share in abundance with his grandchildren, whom his daughter Martha was providing in increasing numbers. The Randolphs had made a habit of moving the four miles from their home at Edgehill to Monticello whenever Jefferson was at home, and by 1809 and his retirement they resided there permanently. Thus many happy hours were spent by all on the west lawn—all, that is, except for Anne, who, at the advanced age of seventeen, had married and moved away. In May 1811 her grandfather wrote her, "Nothing new has happened in our neighborhood since you left us. The houses and trees stand where they did. The flowers come forth like the belles of the day, have their short reign of beauty and splendor, and retire like them to the more interesting office of reproducing their like. The hyacinths and tulips are off the stage, the Irises are giving place to the Belladonnas, as this will to the Tuberoses &c."[3]

Jefferson's ideas always outstripped his ability to put them into practice. Monticello, after all, was a working plantation that from 1809 until his death in 1826 was his sole source of income. Improvements of his fields, mills, canals, and roads, not to mention his nailery, kept him almost fully occupied. Seeds and bulbs were added to his gardens, but the major planting at Monticello was finished.

By then he had several "firsts" to his credit: the creation of his grove on the north slope of his mountain, an eighteen-acre tract that was probably the first arboretum in this country; his nursery of forest trees, which was probably also the first of its kind; with his "moldboard of least resistance" he initiated the standardization of farm equipment; with his flocks of sheep he began the modern breeding program in the United States of that animal.

His energies were then diverted to landscaping Poplar Forest. The house, begun in 1806, was first occupied by him in 1809; but not until 1816 was it respectable enough for the female members of his family, whose presence was indispensable to his happiness. When Martha could not find time away from her brood still at home, a pair of granddaughters were his companions. Jeff, oldest after Anne, had an additional reason to go to Poplar Forest: His grandfather increasingly depended on him on farm matters. By 1815, when Jeff was twenty-three, he had taken over the supervision of Monticello and by 1821 would do the same at Poplar Forest.

Jefferson had begun an orchard in Bedford in 1782. Later he added bush fruits and grapes with a bed for tomatoes, lettuce, and asparagus. By 1811, with public office forever behind him and his octagonal house in its final stages of construction, he began landscaping. His imaginative use of a variety of trees and shrubs is matched only by their numbers—25 of this, 64 of that, not to mention the 190 tulip poplars, the tree for which the plantation had been named many years before Jefferson's ownership. By 1819 he had completed a second landscaping extravaganza.

He was not concerned solely with his own properties in his later years. He was undoubtedly the prime mover behind an organization that first met on May 5, 1817: the Ablemarle Agriculture Society. At this meeting Jefferson was one of five men appointed to prepare the rules and regulations of the organization. After consulting with his fellow members, he drew up a platform outlining "objects for the attention and Enquiry of the Society." Typically Jeffersonian, it is concise but thorough. While some of the details were not implemented, the plan was otherwise what actually transpired during the remainder of the nineteenth century. The history of the Society, however, more properly belongs to James Madison, its first president.

In this year, though, Jefferson was seventy-four, and what

energies were left to him were directed to an even larger under-taking. His last major kindness to American farming and garden-ing was, again typically, involved with education. He established the University of Virginia, which was original both in its design and in Jefferson's insistence of the place botany should occupy in the curriculum.

The buildings were fashioned into an academic village con-sisting of a central rotunda, ten pavilions (with classrooms below and faculty quarters above), and student housing enclosing an area of lawn on three sides. Six hotels and lodging facilities for additional students completed the village. More important, the landscaping and buildings were planned at the same time to form a unified whole. No one who sees Thomas Jefferson's university could mistake it for any other. Although the lawn is its central feature, the garden areas he designed for the back of the buildings that surround it are national treasures individually and collec-tively. He died before they could be planted, but the gardens as reconstructed are based on what he must have had in mind. His landscaping genius for the small formal garden has never been surpassed.

Naturally this dedicated botanist would plan for his university to have a botanical garden and a school of botany. Jefferson laid forth plans for both. For the first he chose an appropriate site opposite the rotunda, and a garden did occupy this space until construction of Cabell Hall destroyed it and the vista he had thought important to his overall design. The school of botany had a different fate. The professor to whom Jefferson assigned the task of creating one already had a crowded schedule, and he was not enthusiastic about adding to his duties. When Jefferson died soon after this proposal was presented, the idea died as well.

Virginians were the poorer for it, but the ex-president had already made his point about the importance of botanical education when he helped form the Albemarle Agriculture Society.

Jefferson summed up his thoughts on the subject with these words written in 1811:

> I have often thought that if heaven had given me choice of my position and calling, it should have been on a rich spot of earth, well watered, and near a good market for the productions of the garden. No occupation is so delightful to me as the culture of the earth, and no culture comparable to that of the garden. Such a variety of subjects, some one always coming to perfection, the failure of one thing repaired by the success of another, and instead of one harvest a continued one through the year. Under a total want of demand except for our family table, I am still devoted to the garden. But though an old man, I am but a young gardener.[4]

James Madison
1809-17

In politics the life of James Madison most visibly paralleled that of his dear friend Thomas Jefferson, eight years his senior. On a more practical level was their common love for and appreciation of farming as a career.

In 1802 Madison wrote Horatio Gates, gracefully declining an invitation to visit the general, "In my relaxation from this place [Washington] I am obliged to keep in mind that I am a farmer and am willing to flatter myself that my farm will be the better for my presence."[1] Jefferson had no thoughts of flattery when he called Madison the best farmer in the world.

Madison held the occupation of farmer in great esteem, as well he might. In his day many of the most prominent men in America were still practicing farmers. In a rural society the remainder of the population accepted the job without question. Some, though, may well have been surprised had they known

Madison's evaluation of their status. In 1792 in the *National Gazette* he wrote, "The class of citizens who provide at once their own food and their own raiment, may be viewed as the most truly independent and happy. They are more: they are the best basis of public liberty, and the strongest bulwark of public safety."[2] Jefferson had said much the same in 1781 in his *Notes on the State of Virginia*.

Nevertheless an agricultural career did not begin seriously for either man until 1793. Jefferson had owned Monticello for more than twenty years, but until then politics had gotten in the way of his being a practicing agriculturist. Madison, who had been born and raised at Montpelier, was after Princeton similarly deprived because of his own involvement in public affairs. As a young man he spent little time at his birthplace, which was ably run by his father, a wealthy, successful planter, and by his younger brother Ambrose.

The Madison land in Orange County, Virginia, had been under development for fewer than 30 years by the time of James Madison's birth in 1751. His grandfather had begun with some 2,300 acres, which by 1757 had been expanded by his father to nearly 4,000 acres. Through trading of assets with other heirs, in addition to the mansion Madison became after his father's death in 1801 the owner of some 5,000 acres divided into 3 farms extending from the banks of the Rapidan River to the top of the Southwest Mountains. The land was of fertile clay and loam, and it responded well to good farming practices.

Although by 1784 Madison owned on Montpelier land 2 farms totaling 560 acres, a gift from his father, his involvement with them competed with his public offices during a period when our Founding Fathers were working diligently to form a new

American government. These farms were not large by Virginia standards, yet they provided Madison with the opportunity of trying in his spare time various agricultural practices and in general managing a plantation of his own. He also speculated in Kentucky lands along with his father and brother; and, with James Monroe, in land in the Mohawk Valley.

In 1793, at the age of forty-two, Madison became responsible for all of Montpelier's fortunes. That year Ambrose died. Now it was up to Congressman Madison to take charge despite his duties in Philadelphia. Fortunately his aging father retained an active interest in farm matters. Correspondence from son to father in this interim period ranges from the need to shift from tobacco to crops less demanding of the soil to possible crop rotations. Improvements such as he had urged upon his father were undertaken by the son after 1797 after his retirement from Congress. Four years later the elder Madison died. By then his namesake was amply prepared to devote undivided attention to this tract of land.

Like Jefferson, Madison was well served at this midlife career shift by a childhood spent observing plantation living and an adulthood devoted to noting and evaluating the scientific agriculture now being practiced by a few farmers at home and abroad and that he himself had been experimenting with on his own acres. We can judge his theoretical if not hands-on knowledge because when he departed for his second term in the Continental Congress in 1787 he left instructions to the managers of each of his two farms. The instructions extended to such details as erosion control.

Both statesmen enjoyed an advantage of inestimable value over most farmers: They were avid readers and had libraries well stocked with books and pamphlets on agriculture and natural history. As early as 1784, for example, Madison wrote to Jefferson that he "[had] Buffon," although which volumes of this French naturalist's *Historie naturelle* (they ran to forty-four in all) he did not say.

Madison and Jefferson had met in Williamsburg in 1776, where both attended the Virginia Constitutional Convention as delegates. (Their friendship endured uninterrupted for half a century until the latter's death.) Madison, who was but twenty-five in 1776 and four years out of Princeton, had already displayed his interest in politics. Despite the hectic times that followed the initial meeting, within eight years, Madison acquired, along with a political education, sufficient knowledge about farming to confidently write his friend about the cinch bug in the wheat and the high prices of tobacco and the insects pests thereof. He also touched on the fact that tobacco production would move west, where the richness of the soil and good climate favored it. With this latter observation Madison was far ahead of his peers, many of whom still clung tenaciously to the idea that Virginia would retain a monopoly on the weed.

Madison was a very private man who kept his interests, except for politics, mostly to himself. He occasionally touched on agricultural matters with others, but to learn his thinking and activities in this field it is necessary to rely on the correspondence between him and the one person he confided in: Jefferson. From these letters it is clear that the younger man kept pace with his mentor's interests. For example, in addition to apples and cranberries, Madison in 1788 sent a box of plants to Paris, where Jefferson was serving as Minister Plenipotentiary to France. Jefferson commented, "They are well chosen, as to the species, for this country," indicating the depth of Madison's knowledge of the subject despite his never having been abroad. But Madison had forgotten, his friend reminded him, to send a promised catalogue from the Prince's nursery on Long Island. In return Jefferson shipped cork acorns, a legume called St. Foin, and peas, all of which Madison was to share with Jefferson's steward for planting at Monticello.

If their friendship needed solidifying, this would have occurred on a month's trip the two took in 1791 to the northern states as far as Vermont. This trip included a visit to Prince's nursery. We can be sure that the observations on the journey basically dealt with the region's natural history and agriculture. Indeed, whereas while Jefferson reported "the principle scenes of General Burgoyne's misfortunes . . . we were more pleased, however, with the botanical objects which continually presented themselves."[3]

By 1793 Jefferson was seeking Madison's opinion of his new crop rotation scheme. As the former was careful to ask opinions only of men whose judgment he respected, Madison must by then have become an accomplished farmer, at least in theory. Jefferson's reasoning was "As you are now immersed in farming & are among farming people. . . ,"[4] but many men fitted this description. In fact Madison was still a congressman and did not take up full-time residence at Montpelier until he left the capital in 1797. Although he anticipated spending the remainder of his life as a planter, especially after his marriage in 1794, this was not to be. He was home only a year when he found himself serving in the Virginia House of Delegates for a second time.

That same year, 1793, the two men traded information regarding plows and threshing machines. Jefferson in Philadelphia asked Madison at Montpelier to get a supply of Kentucky coffee tree seeds for the American botanist William Bartram, with whom, along with Bartram's father, John, Jefferson had been doing business for years. This botanical chitchat continued back and forth for three decades.

In addition to information on plants and animals, the two men also traded weather records. At Jefferson's behest Madison began keeping a daily weather log in 1784 and kept it up for almost twelve years with the assistance of others when Madison himself was not at home. In this area George Washington had led the way among the presidents with John Adams routinely, if imprecisely, noting rain and sun in his diary.

These pleasant occupations were interrupted again by Madison's years as secretary of state and then by his own presidency. As both Madison and his wife were inclined to gardening, it is hardly surprising that they would take a great interest in the landscaping of the White House, especially because they were then landscaping Montpelier. In his role as Jefferson's secretary of state and her role as a frequent hostess for the president, the couple was thoroughly familiar with the problems involved in making order out of the chaos on the grounds of the President's House. Although there is no indication that Jefferson sought or received suggestions regarding a plan of action from these closest of friends, there is every likelihood that the Madisons, being junior partners, were content to agree to the designs approved by Jefferson.

It is interesting that Benjamin Latrobe, with whom Jefferson had collaborated in producing plans to improve the President's Park, waited only ten days after Madison's inauguration to write the new president that his predecessor had approved them and

had already given the necessary directions before leaving office. Although he knew Madison well and had already consulted with him about changes at the White House, Latrobe, who retained the position of surveyor of public buildings, may well have harbored doubts that Madison would forgo his right to change the landscaping that would be associated with his own term of office. The architect was certainly concerned, based on his prior experience, about the willingness of Congress to appropriate sufficient money to implement his and Jefferson's ideas. The sooner work was started, the more likely it would be completed before other, more important projects loomed.

The number of trees and shrubs and the number of species they represented are vintage Jefferson. Large trees for planting as speciments or in rows ranged from willow oak to sugar maple to elm and horsechestnut. Trees and shrubs chosen for screens included white pine, hemlock, mountain ash, and holly. It was an ambitious list. It certainly impressed Jefferson's former White House coachman and general factotum, Joseph Dougherty. He probably did not recognize all the varieties represented, but with his usual hyperbole he wrote Jefferson two months after Madison's inauguration: "Sir, if you were now at the President's house

Drawing by Benjamin Latrobe, 1811. Bases for eagles appear in a c. 1807 landscape plan. (Library of Congress)

59

you would scarcely know it; the north front is become a wilderness of shrubry and trees."[5]

Jefferson himself would have seen it this way. Indeed, he could see a full-grown tree with only a stake in place. A more sober view was written four years later by a visitor who recorded that the front yard might in time be a garden but was now a very ragged and naked piece of turf.

After the British invasion of the White House grounds in 1814, the mansion burned to the walls with damage limited only because of heavy rains. Whose analysis of the landscaping was correct then became academic. As for the Madisons, they never occupied the White House again, living elsewhere in Washington until the end of the president's term in 1817.

The improvement to the Montpelier estate indicates what could have evolved at the White House without the British contribution. In Madison's youth Montpelier still showed all the signs of a young undertaking: A small house built by his grandfather had been replaced by a somewhat larger one by his father during the boy's childhood, but it was hardly impressive. Outbuildings were thrown up when and where needed without thought as to an overall plan or their appearance from the master's home. Landscaping would come later after a real mansion was built and life settled into the routine of a gentleman farmer on his country estate. Indeed, the transformation by Madison ongoing from 1797 could not be called complete until he retired to Montpelier in 1817.

Considering his extensive library and reading habits, his close friendship with that ardent gardener Thomas Jefferson, and his personal observations of gardens such as Monticello's, William Bartram's, Mt. Vernon's, and Gunston Hall's, it is hardly surprising that Madison would go forth and do likewise. Knowing that as the eldest son he would inherit his father's house, he may well have thought about landscaping the estate when he married in 1794, if not before, even though his life until then had been lived mostly in boarding houses rather than at his father's home. He had, after all, bought eighty maple trees at William Prince's nursery on his trip there in 1791 as well as vegetable and flower seeds the same year from Philadelphia.

Madison began with a magnificent view. On a clear day the Blue Ridge Mountains, some thirty miles away, could be seen from almost every part of the estate. This backdrop alone was worth a fortune. However, the house itself had to be attended to first. Initial renovation and enlargement of the home of his parents (itself long under construction) began in 1797 when in March Madison returned to Montpelier with the thought that he had completed his public service and could look forward to a lifetime of farming. He no doubt made plans for the landscaping as well during this period. The French wife of Dr. William Thornton (designer of the U.S. Capitol), who visited Montpelier in 1802, wrote that the grounds were then being developed and when completed, she forecast, would rival the most beautiful of English country seats.

However, progress was slow. A British diplomat who visited in 1807 later recalled, "There are some very fine woods about Montpelier, but no pleasure grounds, though Mr. Madison talks of some day laying out space for an English park, which he might render very beautiful from the easy graceful descent of his hills into the plains below." After commenting on the disinclination of Virginia ladies to face the summer heat outdoors, he continued, "A pleasure ground, too, to be kept in order, would in fact be very expensive, and all hands are absolutely wanted for the plantation."[6]

Madison persisted nonetheless, and Margaret Bayard Smith of Washington recorded this description of an August 1828 visit: "The whole house . . . is surrounded with an extensive lawn, as green as in spring; the lawn is enclosed with fine trees, chiefly forest, but interspersed with weeping willows and other ornamental trees, all of most luxuriant growth and vivid verdure. It was a beautiful scene!" Mrs. Smith might also have commented on the artfully placed groves of trees that screened the farm buildings and slave quarters, the garden temple (placed over the ice house) and the ha-ha, a concealed ditch to prevent farm animals from wondering on the grounds.

The effect must have been especially dramatic, considering Mrs. Smith's description of her party's journey from Monticello (which she had first seen in 1809) to Montpelier. She continues, "We travelled about thirty miles, generally through woods and up and down steep hills . . . after having lost ourselves in the mountain road which leads thro' a wild woody tract of ground and wandering for some time in Mr. Madison's domain, which seemed to us interminable, we at last reached his hospitable mansion."[7] (Interestingly, a British diplomat who traveled the same route in 1807 called the ride very delightful, and the Madisons traveled it without hesitation; also, this near-total isolation, if one is to believe Mrs. Smith, did not prevent hordes of visitors from arriving.)

The Madison family, of course, required food and flowers too for visual enjoyment. Of these there were many kinds, especially roses. With his interest in plants well known, Madison, like Jefferson, was the recipient of many gifts both of American and European origin.

The Madisons were also fortunate in having a French gardener, Beazee, who is remembered for having designed a terraced, horseshoe-shaped garden, said to have been inspired by the seat placement in the House of Representatives, in which Madison had served so long. It was edged, as so many gardens of the period were, with boxwood. Half of the original nearly four-acre expanse remains in gardens. Some of the trees also survive from the Madison era.

Along with the usual vegetables, Montpelier boasted a grand variety of fruit trees, which were supplemented by strawberries and grapes. Madison himself took a particular interest in the latter. Like Jefferson, Madison favored the establishment of a domestic wine industry.

Montpelier was of course made possible by the bounty of its agriculture. Madison's inclination—or, more correctly, sense of responsibility—to encourage similar good farming everywhere in America extended to organizations as well. Although agricultural societies had been formed earlier, it was not until the winter of 1802–3, under Jefferson's presidency, that a central agricultural society was formed. Madison, the secretary of state, was elected its president. This honor shows well the perception of practicing farmers of the secretary's knowledge of the subject and the esteem in which his agricultural peers held him. When it came time to name a president for the newly formed Albermarle Agricultural Society, Madison was the only possible choice as long as Jefferson himself declined the post.

May 12, 1818, is the date on which the first broad-ranging environmental policy in America was prescribed. Madison wrote and delivered a lengthy speech, the basic message of which was: Man is an integral part of his environment. By attempting to dominate it man has and will continue to come only to grief. He must learn to work within the constrictions of the natural world, not act as though he was lord over it. Madison saw very clearly that man can seemingly ignore this precondition to his long-term existence only when human populations remain small.

Madison served as president of the Albemarle Society for seven years. He saw that agriculture must also be included in the curricula of colleges and universities. For America, at least, this was a revolutionary idea, but then Madison and Jefferson, now deeply involved in establishing the University of Virginia, were both prime instigators of an earlier revolutionary period. At the university, Madison served first as a member of the board of visitors, then as rector, succeeding Jefferson.

There is no doubt that Madison, despite his extensive and brilliant contributions to the political field, was still basically a farmer. At the time he left Washington for good, he wrote that his primary goal was to become a fixture on his farm, where he expected many pleasures. There can be no doubt, either, about his abilities in that occupation. For example, according to his attorney general, Richard Rush, Madison had the reputation of being an excellent farm manager. Despite this ability, he never realized the profits he could rightfully have expected, for after his presidential terms the Virginia Piedmont economy began a long, slow decline. His own habits of thrift and lack of ostentation were negated too by debts incurred by Payne Todd, his wife's son by her first marriage, and the constant stream of visitors to Montpelier.

With his income totally dependent on his farm after he left public service, Madison fought a holding action, selling his lands in Kentucky, stock, and other assets. He was even forced to mortgage nearly half of his Montpelier property. As with his friends Jefferson and Monroe, his dream of making farming a viable if not prosperous profession came to naught.

James Monroe

1817-25

Presidential biographers seldom note their subjects' views of botanical matters; political events dominate the research and hence the written results. In the case of James Monroe, a prospective biographer has an additional handicap: Monroe himself left almost nothing for the record about his agricultural or horticultural activities. His farm records are gone. He was not a diary keeper, as George Washington and both the Adamses were. His autobiography contains little personal information except as it relates to the public affairs with which he was involved. His letters were almost exclusively about political matters. Even with his mentor and longtime dear friend Thomas Jefferson, Monroe ignored botanical chitchat of common interest. Jefferson in turn respected the younger man's inclinations and kept his own references to farming and horticulture to a bare minimum.

One might conclude that Monroe was not really concerned

with the topic, that his interest extended only as far as the income (much needed) his fields could provide. This is not an accurate assessment. His library of some 3,000 volumes included a 30-volume edition of *Historie naturelle* by the great French naturalist Buffon and works by other men such as the French naturalist Baron Georges Curier and the English scientist Erasmus Darwin. Monroe, in fact, was well read in these subjects. Although his passion was politics, if asked what his occupation was he would have answered "farmer." When the pressures of his various diplomatic and political offices became too intense, he found his solace in his fields. This was not just a matter of personal satisfaction, for like his Virginia compatriots Washington, Jefferson, and Madison he was greatly interested in agricultural reform and followed the lead of these elders by personally doing something about it.

As with our other early presidents, Monroe came from a farming background. He was born in Westmoreland County, the birthplace of Washington. Like this gentleman, Monroe spent his adult years elsewhere. Westmoreland County, one of the first areas settled in Virginia, had known some of the colony's greatest wealth, being a prime producer of that often lucrative crop tobacco. By the time of Washington's early manhood the fortunes of the county had declined. Only the very largest land owners (who frequently held land elsewhere as well) could afford to retain their ancestral seats.

Monroe's father had owned fewer than 500 acres, which he left to James, his eldest son. As a youngster James had enjoyed the usual pursuits of plantation life: riding and hunting. He had also developed a keen interest in the agriculture upon which his family had so long depended for income and that surrounded him in his own youth. He could not have failed to learn also of the problems his home county was experiencing with regard to agriculture. This carefree life came to an abrupt end when his father died. Monroe, age sixteen, began college at William and Mary under the guidance of Judge Joseph Jones, his uncle.

For those living in Williamsburg, the year 1774 was an especially momentous one. Had the times been more peaceful, Monroe might well have followed an agricultural career. Given the circumstances, however, a more natural field of study was politics, along with a healthy dose of military life. For a teenager who had already perfected his riding and hunting skills and knew country conditions very well, the more immediate prospect of becoming a soldier was irresistible. Monroe served his country with distinction, first in the military and then in politics. Through it all, however, he never forgot his agricultural heritage.

In Williamsburg by 1780, at age twenty-two Monroe had befriended a man who was to channel his life to future honors. Because of this man Monroe formed a friendship with a second who also significantly shaped his life. The first patriot was Thomas Jefferson, the second James Madison. The three men soon began a collaboration unique in American history that lasted until their deaths. The collaboration was not only political but also in their individual fields. Common problems there fostered solutions arrived at by three of the best minds in America.

Monroe at the time of his introduction to these men was in need of an estate upon which to build his life and fortune. In order to advance his social and political ambitions (in 1787 he was elected to the Virginia House of Delegates) he wished to find a home in the Piedmont for in 1780 Virginia's capital was relocated to Richmond. Like other men looking to the future, Monroe was also eager to speculate in land. As a war veteran, by 1783 he had received a land bounty of more than 5,000 acres in Kentucky. Soon he secured a government grant conveying to him fee-simple title to over 100,000 acres in that state.

In 1786, at the age of twenty-eight, Monroe got married. His marriage added to the pressure he felt to find a plantation suited to his immediate needs. He found one two years later—800 acres of land that later came to be the site of the University of Virginia. The deal included a house in Charlottesville. He had no available cash for the asking price of £2,500, but the owner was willing to accept some of Monroe's Kentucky acreage as payment.

Early in 1789 Monroe sent servants, horses, and equipment to begin his venture. The young couple did not themselves move until late August. Their arrival predated by several months Jefferson's return to America from France. The latter stayed only briefly at Monticello (just a few miles from Monroe's new estate) as he soon began duty as president Washington's secretary of state. Nonetheless the two friends were now officially neighbors both in Albemarle and in Washington, where Monroe was serving as a senator. To emphasize his commitment to his new estate, Monroe began building a house on it.

He must have proceeded with his plans with some trepidation. His legal career, launched at the time of his marriage, suffered from the unsteady income experienced by most new lawyers. His first crops were disappointments, and he fretted about the quality of these particular acres and his inability to find enough time to supervise them properly. He even toyed with the idea of abandoning the estate in favor of a more productive one.

In the spring and summer of 1793 he was home to personally command his forces, and, with weather that cooperated, he managed a bumper crop. His new house had proceeded as planned, and guests could be suitably lodged (thus fulfilling an important prerequisite for plantation hospitality). With life running smoothly, Monroe, following the example set by so many of his peers, decided to buy more land. The Charlottesville area was showing its kinder sides, and Jefferson and Monticello continued to be a powerful magnet. Monroe bought adjacent to the Jefferson estate a 3,500-acre tract that he planned for his permanent residence. An 800-acre tract was hardly sufficient for the lifestyle he intended. He was only in his mid-thirties, and life was rosy and everything possible.

In 1794 Monroe began a new phase in his career; he was appointed minister to France by President Washington. Although Monroe managed to retain his strong sense of duty to his country throughout his life and craved the political scene, the financial sacrifices he made as a result of this service abroad should have warned him of things to come. His predecessors in such posts provided examples. His expenses proved considerably more than the new government provided. Meanwhile his lands at home suffered in his absence. An overseer in charge in Albemarle under the general direction of Monroe's aging uncle was no substitute for his own presence.

Monroe's interests were also addressed by his neighbor Jefferson, who had left his post as secretary of state and arrived home in early January 1794. His own farms and his finances were both in a deplorable state for the same reasons Monroe would soon encounter. The older man was well aware of the hazards of trying to farm long distance and with periodic uncooperative weather and markets. Nevertheless, facts had to be faced. He reported to Monroe in Philadelphia in March 1794 that there had been very few plowing days since mid-January, so that farmers had never been so far behind in their preparations for planting. Jefferson would make similar reports after the younger man went abroad.

While he was no doubt frustrated by such adverse news, the diplomat, far from home, was no doubt gratified that his mentor was willing to act in any area that was under human control. Jefferson wrote in May 1796 that he had made arrangements to have fruit trees, grown in his own nursery especially for Monroe, transplanted to the latter's new estate adjacent to Monticello. Remembering his own sojourn abroad, he pointed out to his friend the trees should be planted so "they may be growing during your absence." He added, "Do not fail to send over the Apricot-peche. Bartram would receive & plant it, and then furnish new plants."[1] William Bartram carried on his father John's varied botanical enterprises from the family farm outside Philadelphia.

Monroe was absent four years, returning home in August 1798. His fields had suffered in the interval, and his Charlottesville house probably seemed more cramped than he had remembered it; in fact, he must have been appalled at what he perceived as his scanty accommodations. The hunger to start building on his new tract overcame any reservations he might have felt about his financial conditions.

This acreage, first referred to by Monroe as the "lower plantation," passed through a phase of being called Highland (sometimes in the plural) before being known as Ashlawn. Monroe built a one-story frame house of some six rooms on the property into which the family moved in December 1799. He intended it to be temporary, until he could afford something more grand. This was not to be, although he lived on this estate until he retired to Loudon County after leaving the presidency in 1825.

Monroe was busy planning his first winter home. Recognizing at last that diplomatic and political posts would cost, not make, him money, he cleared more land, thus allowing him to increase his tobacco crop by 20,000 pounds. Considering that Jefferson had already abandoned tobacco as a mainstay of his Albemarle property, favoring since 1794 a crop rotation based on small grains, corn, and clover, it is surprising that Monroe—fifteen years younger and theoretically in a better position to plant for the long run—did not follow suit. His debts must have weighed heavily upon him to so blatantly and short-sightedly expand his tobacco production.

His farming career was interrupted once again by a second mission to France in 1803. Jefferson, now president, chose his young friend to assist Robert Livingston in the delicate negotiations that resulted in the Louisiana Purchase. Monroe spent four more years abroad, in London and Madrid. If we had nothing to depend on except his own writings, it would seem that his time was devoted exclusively to diplomatic matters. Thanks to Jefferson, we know that Monroe turned to agricultural interests at least once during this period. Jefferson wrote in May 1807,

> The sole object in writing . . . is to add another little commission to the one I had formerly troubled you with. It is to procure for me 'a machine for ascertaining the resistance of ploughs or carriages, invented and sold by Winlaw, in Margaret street, Cavendish Square.' It will cost, I believe, four or five guineas, which shall be replaced here instanter on your arrival."[2]

Neither Jefferson nor Madison, now secrtary of state, had time to supervise Highland, and the manager Monroe chose proved inefficient. A major blow to Monroe was the sale to creditors, by the manager, of Monroe's original Charlottesville property for £1,500, a sum much less than Monroe thought the property worth. Like Jefferson, Monroe seems to have been slow to recognize that property appraisements had begun a decline that would last until their respective deaths. After decades of severe land abuse, Virginia's Piedmont was now feeling the full effects of lowered productivity that the Tidewater region had earlier. It was easier for a man to pull up stakes and move west to start over on virgin soil. Despite what they saw or heard about what Jefferson was doing in his fields, local farmers, Monroe reported, were amused at first when he too planted clover and covered his fields with plaster of paris. As had the doubters who scoffed at Jefferson, Monroe's critics had to acknowledge that this new way of farming produced good results. Trying out the plan on their own farms was another matter.

Monroe showed himself to be an agricultural innovator in grape culture too. Like Jefferson's before him, Monroe's experiences in France acquainted him firsthand not only with the virtues of French wines but also with how the world's best viticulturists grew their raw product. Monroe therefore imported vines from Bordeaux to begin his own vineyard. Once again politics intruded, and this venture too was put on hold. The vineyard must have been at least modestly successful, though, for in January 1816, while Monroe was secretary of state, Jefferson asked his absent neighbor if a man proficient in the art who would soon be in the neighborhood could do the pruning of Monroe's vines and take the trimmings to increase the number of varieties already growing at Monticello. For Monroe, the interest in viticulture remained.

As president he served French wines but also native types, especially wine made from the south's scuppernong grape.

By 1811, when Monroe was asked to be Madison's secretary of state, he could with some certainty plot his own future. Jefferson had been Washington's secretary of state, and Madison had succeeded to the presidency from that post. Monroe foresaw that the remainder of his career could center on the national capital if he so chose. The fact that the trip from there to Albemarle was arduous and lengthy caused Monroe to pay more interest now to his more recently acquired property, Oak Hill, in Loudon County, just thirty miles from the capital.

Monroe wrestled with his problem. His heart seems to have remained at Highland. Yet he recognized the advantages of Oak Hill: its closeness to Washington and its potentially better soils (unfullfilled because of the unskilled management of his brother Andrew). But Monroe was unable to sell the Loudon property; perhaps he should try selling Highland? Each year his financial woes increased. Nevertheless, like his peers in Virginia and their fathers and grandfathers before them, he saw land as the only feasible and acceptable way out of his difficulties.

Despite his dismal financial status, Monroe, now elevated to the highest office his country had to offer, in 1817 thought of building a bigger house at Oak Hill. The original was a six-room frame building that during his presidency was enlarged to a spacious home. It was set in a grove of locusts, poplars, and oaks with views of rolling farm lands toward the Blue Ridge Mountains. These features, together with views also of the Catoctin Hills and of Sugar Loaf Mountain, appear to have satisfied his aesthetic demands. The only trees he planted were oaks, one from each

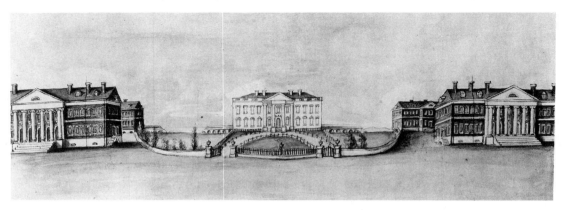

Drawn by Baroness Hyde de Neuville, 1820. Note that east and west wings do not extend to State and Treasury (left) *and War and Navy* (right), *as planned.* (Library of Congress)

state in the union, presented to him by congressmen from the respective states.

Monroe also continued with improvements at Highland and even thought at one point to retire there after the conclusion of his second term. Basically, though, his life was on hold in terms of his agricultural interests. If Virginia land prices had been sliding before, the Panic of 1819 accelerated the decline, so he did what he could with the land he had.

At the White House he was faced with similar financial restraints in resolving the disorder he found at his doorstep there. The President's Park consisted of some sixty acres. This included what is now Lafayette Park, the site of the mansion itself, and the slope to Tiber Creek. Although only a few acres around the house were designated for the president's personal use, the entire Park demanded attention.

Monroe began his term of office sensibly enough—from a horticultural point of view—by hiring late in 1817 the Frenchman Charles Bizet, to whom he gave the somewhat ostentatious title "Gardener to the President of the U. States." Bizet's salary was $450 a year. Unfortunately, the record of his activities is scant. Although a vegetable garden was of course necessary, Monroe

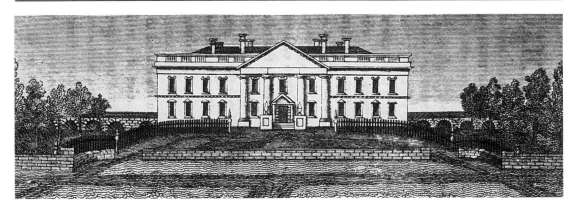

apparently did not feel the same about flowers or other purely ornamental plants. He had shown no interest in them before. More basic work needed doing, for there was still considerable evidence of the damage done by the British to governmental buildings. To help rectify the damage, in 1818 Congress made an appropriation of $10,000 for improving the President's Park.

Around the mansion itself visitors reported that Ionic pilaster caps, now ruined, littered the yard, as did broken ashlar blocks. Yet instead of clearing this mess, strangely, Monroe seemed more concerned with the fact that Jefferson's stone wall blocked the view of the White House from the north except at the gate. The wall was consequently reduced in height with an iron railing of tall spears replacing the upper stones. To complete the new look, in 1820 the north entrance was redone with iron gates attached to stone piers. Monroe had no problem with the south wall, for the hill on which the mansion sat was sufficiently high to allow an unobstructed view from that direction. The addition of the South Portico to the mansion in 1824 did not spur Monroe into thinking of landscaping possibilities.

As for the grounds, Bizet for all practical purposes had to start from scratch. The trees that Jefferson had planted were

Drawing by George Catlin, c. 1820. Note that North Portico has yet to be built. (Library of Congress)

77

almost all gone, victims of the British invasion and the subsequent rebuilding. Furthermore, grading of the sixty acres had barely begun and, in a day before bulldozers, was slow going. Bizet started with the area north of the house across Pennsylvania Avenue, where, after grading was completed, trees were planted. (By 1824 Pennsylvania Avenue extended through the President's Park in front of the mansion to tie into 15th Street and Pennsylvania Avenue, leading to the Capitol.) Bizet apparently worked from plans developed by Charles Bulfinch, a Boston architect whom Monroe hired in 1818 to finish the Capitol. Bulfinch also developed plans for the White House grounds—plans that are now lost. He seems to have followed Jefferson's idea of planting extensively with trees.

Work ground almost to a halt as the result of the Panic of 1819, two years into Monroe's first term. The president was very conscious of the need to keep governmental expenditures to a minimum. As landscaping was never his forte, we can assume that this lack of progress did not cause Monroe the anguish Jefferson would have experienced. At the end of Monroe's second term extensive grading still remained to be done. Gullies needed filling, and low areas required draining, if not also filling. Load by load, cartmen moved the dirt around. Even with wages based on a load moved the men could physically accomplish only so much with their backs and their shovels. The few shade trees that were planted—each surrounded by a wooden box for protection against wandering livestock—were a tribute to the men's labors.

If Monroe mourned his lack of progress with the White House grounds, he left no record of it. In 1825, when John Quincy Adams assumed office, Monroe, his political ambitions now apparently sated, returned his attention to his farms. Indeed, even had he not found contentment in doing so his finances would not have permitted any other course, for he was on the verge of total ruin. In time presidential pensions would ease the transition back to private life. Fortunately his abilities as a farmer were considerable, and he had the excellent example of his dear friends Jefferson and Madison as inspiration. Monroe returned to Oak Hill to rescue what he could of his crumbling fortunes.

Oak Hill was planted mostly with grains grown in rotation, with clover, fallows, and gypsum helping out to keep his land productive. Monroe, who had 360 sheep in 1817, planned to increase this number to 1,000 because of his fine meadows. The ex-president's days were filled with planting, threshing, fencing, and shearing. He joined with Jefferson and Madison in the project of creating the University of Virginia and regularly attended Board of Visitors meetings almost until his death. This was the major exception to his farm activities. His idyllic life was marred only by his crushing need to cope with his debts.

In the summer of 1825 Monroe attempted to sell Highland, deciding at last to retire to Oak Hill. The offers made for the estate were much below the appraisers' assessments, and he withdrew the property from the market. In desperation he sold 900 acres of the best land there, although this action would decrease his chance of selling the remainder at an acceptable price. The following year he attempted to sell this part at auction. When bids did not come in at his minimum price, he relinquished all but 707 acres to the Bank of the United States in lieu of payment of a $25,000 loan. Sale of Highland slaves paid off another debt.

Jefferson, in similar dire straits at this time, finally agreed to a lottery scheme proposed by his grandson to alleviate the old man's debts. Monroe turned to Congress on the basis of expenses he had incurred while serving his country but was never paid. While neither man succeeded in becoming solvent, Monroe did fare somewhat better.

After Monroe's wife died in 1830, he was no longer able to live at Oak Hill because of age and a grief that prostrated him. When he left his Loudon County home to live with his daughter in New York, he determined to sell it, but death intervened. Like Jefferson and John Adams before him, Monroe died on July 4— just five years after these two illustrious founders.

John Quincy Adams
1825-29

Considering his own reluctance as a child to be anything but a farmer and considering the veneration in which he clearly held agriculture, it is surprising that John Adams so artfully prevented his own first born, John Quincy, from experiencing its pleasures and rewards. Like his father before him, John Adams had a plan for this son, reinforced by a Revolutionary War background. The plan was concurred in wholeheartedly by Abigail Adams. John Quincy, their son, was to be trained as a statesman. His mentors included not only his well-versed and experienced father and mother but also Benjamin Franklin, George Washington, and Thomas Jefferson as well. With his own very able mentality to assist, John Quincy's diplomatic career was long and distinguished, as was his political career with the exception of the four presidential years. Between 1794 and 1848, the year of his death, John Quincy held almost every political and diplomatic post America had to offer.

Like his predecessors in the office of president, John Quincy had a deeply felt understanding of an American's responsibilities. His public career stood at the top of his list of priorities, even above wife and children. It was not until he was older that his horizons broadened to include various phases of botany and science in general. He had been sated until then by history, literature, philosophy, even painting, sculpture, and efforts with the flute.

But by his later years, especially in regard to his very active role in the establishment of the Smithsonian Institution, it can be said without hesitation that no one since Benjamin Franklin and Thomas Jefferson had done as much to advance the cause of science in America. John Quincy became a tireless advocate of the construction of astronomical observatories, a national university, and scientific explorations—all of which he proposed upon assuming the presidency. His promotion of forest trees was also unusual for his day. New silvicultural efforts in Europe won his admiration, and he chafed at his inability to light a fire of enthusiasm under his fellow citizens to improve American dedication to planting the utilitarian tree as well as the ornamental.

For these legacies we can thank his enthusiasms while president. However, despite his training in European courts and American legislative bodies, John Quincy seemed in some respects to have few talents for diplomatic and political life. Perhaps he was not even particularly suited for the role of a Harvard professor, a post he held from 1806 to 1809, although he was by temperament and long habit a scholar who read and spoke Latin, Greek, French, German, Dutch, and Italian. Of charisma he had none, if compared with other members of the Adams family. His oratorical and general conversational abilities were, except with family members and close friends, on a par with Jefferson's, which is to say they were virtually nil. Yet these were not insurmountable handicaps for aspiring politicians in the days prior to radio and television.

John Quincy served only one term as president, but nonetheless he had a highly successful political career, in Congress as a senator from 1803–1809 and a representative from 1831–1848, and especially as James Monroe's secretary of state, during which period he completed Jefferson's work of expanding the nation's boundaries from the Atlantic to the Pacific. Being president was another matter. Because he was a largely invisible one, most Americans today recognize nothing about him except the fact that his name is the same as John Adams's except with a "Quincy" in the middle.

Nevertheless he left an important legacy to those of us concerned with agriculture and horticulture. Coupled with the scholar's reliance on books was the enthusiasm of the dirt gardener. John Quincy never worried about his fingernails or that some might find it amusing that the president of the United States should range over the woods in pursuit of acorns (as he related to his son George Washington Adams in 1828). In order to plant them in Washington John Quincy publicly retrieved several acorns from under an oak in Baltimore that had been struck by enemy musket bullets during the War of 1812. The local men who accompanied him must have spread that story far and wide. To John Quincy, the budding forester, the act was as natural as breathing itself. He was truly gratified that the Washington woods contained five species of oak and saw to it that he secured and planted acorns from each.

What had driven John Quincy to botanical matters were the

barbs he experienced as chief executive. Politically he was a minority president whose election was due to the House of Representatives because Andrew Jackson had had a plurality although not a majority of the electoral vote. Washington's weather and social life did not agree with John Quincy. His marital life, never the resounding success his parents had enjoyed, did little to sustain him emotionally. His health, reflecting the aches and pains of so many Americans of the age, became far from good. Finding his usual refuge—his books and his pen—no longer a source of refreshment as they had once been, he consciously expanded his physical activities. He increased the length of his walks and his horseback rides while his swimming feats became legendary—and he began a serious love affair with plants.

He wrote in his diary in June 1827, two years after assuming the presidency, "My health and spirits droop, and the attempt to sustain them by . . . botany, the natural history of trees, and the purpose of naturalizing exotics is almost desperate."[1] He pursued this new occupation at the White House, where he was then spending most of his time. He was not satisfied, though, with just those grounds. While he had always been drawn to the family hearth in Quincy, Massachusetts, this birthplace now assumed an additional importance, for it provided him with good and sufficient land all his own on which to pursue his new dedication to planting and experimentation.

When John Quincy arrived at the White House as president the scene was still a rather stark one. Planning of the grounds had not begun until Thomas Jefferson's term of office, and little had been accomplished then. James Madison had had the War of 1812 and the destruction of the new government's public buildings by the British to contend with. James Monroe was beset by the need to finish the rebuilding.

The White House John Quincy entered was flanked by two low wings that included space for a stable and a small dairy. Immediately to the north of the mansion were only three private residences and a church. Across Pennsylvania Avenue and the President's Park there was open country west of 16th Street. To the south beyond the area planned for the formal gardens by Jefferson was a two-block-wide meadow that sloped to the river, a few hundred yards away. A cow or two kept for milk and butter for presidential use grazed there, as did a few sheep whose major duty was to help mow the grass. John Quincy did little to enhance the building itself, but he made his mark on these grounds. Large numbers of plants were purchased or collected by the president and others to adorn the largely barren landscape. On the south lawn an elm planted as a seedling by John Quincy endured until 1991.

His actual experience with gardening and farming had been delayed until his maturity, schooling and travel having previously consumed his days. He had purchased the original part of the Adams family home acres in 1803 at age thirty-six to provide his parents with much-needed cash. His father and mother were no longer in need of either the house John Adams had been born in or the adjacent house in which John Quincy had been born, for they had resided since 1787 in their big mansion nearby. John Quincy then commenced some hands-on experience with gardening at his birthplace as well as at the house he occupied while a senator in Washington. His life, however, was again interrupted by service abroad and then as secretary of state. Before he became president, therefore, John Quincy had learned some basics but no more, especially at his Quincy farm, as he was so seldom there. His serious botanical education was, for all practical purposes, yet to begin.

Not surprisingly, his original gardening goal in 1827 was a nationalistic one, paralleling his goals as secretary of state and president. His garden was to contain a collection of American plants, most notably trees. He followed Jefferson's landscape plan and located the main ornamental garden, ultimately of two acres' extent, to the right of the south entrance gate. More growing space was achieved by the use of cold frames to the south and north of the main garden. The garden itself was fenced with parallel boards and included a cistern to catch rain water. This was supplemented by a pump at the well serving the nearby Treasury Building. Jefferson's Treasury vault, gutted by British fire, became the garden tool house. While the president appreciated these physical features, he had another treasure in the person of John Ousley (probably an Englishman), whom the president had hired by the beginning of August 1825 to replace Charles Bizet, who had not distinguished himself under President Monroe. Ousley served his employer—and future presidents—well.

At this period of his life John Quincy could look back over the years with some bemusement. He had come from a background of farming and horticulture; John and Abigail Adams's lives were founded on both. Their son would write wistfully in 1833, almost two years into another career, this time as a member of the House of Representatives, "My natural propensity was to raise trees, fruit and forest, from the seed. I had it in my early youth, but the course of my life deprived me of the means of pursuing the bent of my inclination. . . . Had my life been spent in the country, and my experiments commenced while I was at college, I should now have a large fruit-garden, flourishing orchards of native fruit, and very valuable forests; instead of which I have a nursery of about half an acre of ground, half full of seedlings, from five years to five days old, bearing for the first time perhaps twenty peaches, and a few blossoms of apricots and cherries; and hundreds of seedlings of the present year perishing from day to day before my eyes."[2] The cry was real, but what Adams suffered from the most was an inability to recognize that first and foremost he was, and always had been, a political man.

Nevertheless when he wrote those words he must also have thought back to those terrible days midway through his presidency when he understood that, during this period at least, his qualifications and the requirements of the office did not match, especially given the temperament of the times. By 1826, looking to escape his increasingly unhappy situation in office, he wrote, "As on many occasions, I have betaken myself to a pursuit which already absorbs too much of my time, and would, if indulged, soon engross it all."[3]

He *had* been unobservant. He wrote in his diary on April 9, 1827, after noting the unfolding of new leaves on the trees, "The variety in their manner of vegetating is so remarkable that I am humiliated by the heedlessness with which I have suffered this process to pass at least fifty times before my eyes without bestowing a thought upon it."[4]

The immediate jolt to action had been a resolution by the House of Representatives requiring the preparation of a manual concerning the cultivation of silkworms in preparation for the establishment of a silk industry in America. This idea had been pursued since the earliest colonial period as official policy. It had come to nothing despite the personal interest of men like Jefferson. John Quincy also became concerned about reviving on the east coast a formerly abundant resource that had been destroyed to a large extent during 200 years of occupation by Europeans—namely forests, live and white oak forests in particular because of their importance to American ship building.

He recognized very well how little he knew about forestry, so characteristically he decided to study books, supplementing this by actual experiments. In his nursery he proposed to concentrate on oaks, hickories, and chestnuts. Within days he had made arrangements with the son of Judge Richard Peters, a leading Philadelphia agriculturist and horticulturist, to send him from the senior Peters's garden chestnuts that had been planted there by that gentleman and George Washington. He acknowledged to his diary that he should have commenced the project thirty years previously but consoled himself that the public would ultimately benefit even if he had not. He pointed out, truthfully, that he never had had a permanent address, by which he meant one from which he never strayed.

It was not until the following spring, though, that he began his silvicultural, even general horticultural, studies in earnest. At his instigation a few books on the subject had been found in London and Paris and were forwarded to Washington. John Quincy could not have helped but be impressed with these foreign volumes. Even this otherwise indefatigable scholar despaired of conquering John Claudius Loudon's *An Encyclopedia of Gardening* (1,240 pages) and his *Encyclopedia of Agriculture* (1,224 pages), not to mention the five treatises Hamel Du Monceau needed to cover the subject of forests. The French botanist André Michaux, who had already made his mark with earlier U.S. presidents, would do so with this one too—although through his son. François-André Michaux's *North American Sylva* was eagerly read by John Quincy. John Evelyn had encouraged his fellow Englishmen in *Sylva* to plant millions of timber trees and encouraged this American president to do the same. With the addition of still more books the poor president found that the more he studied the more questions he had. He complained to his diary, "I believe ten summers of unrelaxing attention will be necessary to accomplish anything useful for posterity, and, after all, it may terminate in disappointment."[5]

On April 24, 1827, John Quincy set forth in earnest on his practical scheme, realizing that he could spend only an hour daily on "this fantastical humor." He and Antonine, his longtime steward, planted nuts of large Pennsylvania walnuts, Quincy walnuts, hazelnuts, and three more of the chestnuts from Judge Peters's son, supplemented by seeds of apple.

Within weeks John Quincy set his sights higher. Perhaps as a result of his new reading agenda, he decided that in addition to an American museum of trees there were foreign trees, fruits, and herbaceous plants that could profitably be introduced in America beyond those staples that had already been imported. His proposed agents were captains of U.S. vessels who visited distant ports. The secretary of the treasury was duly instructed to send every U.S. consul a circular explaining that the president was looking for "forest trees useful as timber; grain of any description; fruit trees; vegetables for the table; esculent roots; and, in short, plants of whatever nature whether useful as food for man or the domestic animals, or for purposes connected with manufacturers or any of the useful arts. . . ."[6] In this he was following the example of Jefferson, who had solicited the support of American consuls at all foreign ports to transmit seeds of the finest fruits and vegetables growing in the host country.

This was followed by pages of instructions of information needed for each plant. These included where the plant was found, the soil it grew in, and insect pests. Additional pages gave detailed instructions regarding how the seeds, roots, and nuts or the plants themselves should be packed to survive a long voyage by sea. John Quincy wanted success in an undertaking few Americans had even thought of, let alone attempted. The ship captains, for their part, must have marveled at their president's boldness to think that many seeds, let alone living trees and shrubs, would survive the ordeal. The president was also perhaps presumptuous in supposing that everyone involved in this feat, from collector to the man who finally delivered the bounty, would do so for free; Congress had provided no money.

But John Quincy's audacity was proven justified. In just three months he got his first shipment, Spanish chestnuts, immediately followed by another box of chestnuts and one of cork oak. He had his son George retrieve them from the customs collector in Boston. The president paid the charges himself. Shrewdly he asked the collector, a farmer and gardener as well, how to keep the chestnuts over winter and authorized George to give the man some nuts in return. This goodwill gesture would ensure enthusiastic treatment of future shipments. Meanwhile George was instructed to divide the remainder, plant some in Quincy, and send the rest to Washington. The president was gratified that other shipments followed on a regular basis. On April 22, 1827, for example, Charles, another son, picked up forty English oak trees, twenty-two buttonwoods, and sixty elms, all saplings, which he took to Quincy. Soon John Quincy was also getting gifts of nuts, seeds, and plants from friends at home and abroad.

Indoors at the White House he busied himself with watching the development of several silkworms. The president wanted to know the life history of the insect that might at last launch a silk industry in America. In addition to these duties he kept almost hourly watch on the development of plants growing in three flower pots. Outdoors he already had put a respectable variety of plants into the ground.

In June 1827 he wrote,

> In this small garden, of less than two acres, there are forest- and fruit-trees, shrubs, hedges, esculent vegetables, kitchen and medicinal herbs, hot-house plants, flowers, and weeds, to the amount, I conjecture, of at least one thousand. One-half of them perhaps are common weeds, most of which have none but the botanical name. I ask the name of every plant I see. Ousley, the gardener, knows almost all of them by their botanical names, but the numbers to be discriminated and recognized are baffling to the memory and confounding to the judgement. From the small patch where the medicinal herbs stand together I plucked this morning leaves of balm and hyssop, marjoram, mint, rue, sage, tansy, tarragon, and wormwood, one-half of which were known to me only by name—the tarragon not even by that.[7]

John Quincy's world was broadening fast.

To keep up with the multitudinous questions that kept occurring to him, he returned again and again to his books. Always an early riser, he sneaked in his botanical reading beginning at the crack of dawn. Then it was out to the garden to make on-the-spot observations of how plants grow. He noted on June 13 that for the past three days he had forgone his usual walk taken for exercise to devote more time to his garden. He was already planning for the preservation of seeds for planting in fall and the following spring. In short, John Quincy Adams was hooked.

He spent two months in Quincy that summer, arriving on August 4. One of the hottest spells in memory descended, leaving him unable even to write. His brief vacation was interrupted by the usual round of callers, but by the twelfth he was solidly back on track with regard to gardening. He had four small wooden tubs made for seedlings and immediately planted five tamarind stones and eight pear seeds in one and five tamarind and six pear seeds in a second. This was to be an experiment to see whether stones and seeds from grafted or budded trees would germinate. His literary sources did not provide an answer.

He was also gratified that at the nursery he had established at his summer home—the original family homestead, which he had bought from his parents in 1803—more "shag-bark walnuts" had come up, making twelve to have done so. He also noted horse-chestnuts and oaks that had germinated but mourned to his diary,

> In this branch of natural history my experiments have commenced so late in life, and are yet so little governed by a system pointing directly to useful ends, that they may perhaps end in mere trifles; but that is not my intention. On the 8th of October, 1804, I planted perhaps forty walnuts in this garden, several of which came up the ensuing summer. One of them was transplanted to the garden of the house where my father was born, and lives, but is not yet in bearing; one only remains on the spot where the nut was planted, and, at the age of twenty-one years, last autumn bore perhaps two hundred nuts. Most of these I planted here and twelve at

Washington, and there are now thirteen of them here and twelve at Washington growing. But last year was my first experiment of planting acorns, and that has been partially successful here, and totally failed at Washington. Colonel Perkins told me yesterday that he thought our pasture white oak, well salted, as good for ship-building as the best live-oak. This is encouragement for me to persevere in my experiments, which I would leave as at once a charge and an inheritance to my children.[8]

In Washington that fall (1827) he planted numerous oaks of several species, hickories, walnuts, chestnuts, persimmons, tulip poplars, and lime as a border around his garden and hoped they would outlast many presidents. He feared they might be up-rooted, but the thought did not deter him.

In early May the following spring, among frequent references to the results of his planting endeavors, he found eighty-two trees growing along the north border, three along the west, with none along the south or east. A sharp frost and a later hailstorm had caused damage if not death to these and fruit trees occupying the garden. Later that month he wrote to his son Charles about nuts he had planted,

They are now coming up, and within the last fortnight upwards of two hundred trees have shown themselves above the surface. I expect with another month to witness the birth of near two hundred more. I shall see little of these myself, but in leaving an infant forest under the eyes of my Successors, I intend it as a memento for them which I hope they will have the means of cherishing.[9]

By summer he had become reconciled to botanical death. He could now afford to be philosophical, for he had more than 700 saplings of some 20 varieties growing at the White House. They were a very necessary tonic to the political disappointment he was experiencing. The trees would be his legacy to the nation he had served all his adult life, and he took pride in that. He could also relish the fact he had contributed at least one positive bit of knowledge by his experiments: Self-planted seeds thrive more vigorously than those planted by man. He noted sadly, though, "The plants which I most cherish are the most apt to disappoint me and die."[10] Mr. Adams had come of age as a gardener.

It is a testimony to his belief in the importance of the presidential office, even though it had not dealt kindly with him personally, that he persevered to such an extent given the response of most of his countrymen to his efforts. A great part of the problem lay not necessarily with his ideas but with his lack of ability to communicate. The highlight of his political courting, in fact, revolved around a tree. Trees were something he knew very well how to deal with. The occasion was the Independence Day celebration of 1828, at which he was to break ground for the Chesapeake and Ohio Canal. His spade at once struck a large submerged tree trunk. He tried several more times without success to come up with a shovelful of earth at the designated spot, whereupon, throwing off his coat, he finally succeeded at the task. The 2,000 spectators roared their approval. This was something they could empathize with. Even John Quincy understood that this small unplanned act was worth all the speeches he had ever made in order to obtain the support of his constituents.

He was not so lucky after he left office. Adherents of Andrew Jackson were determined to exterminate all vestiges of Adams's presence, or so it seemed to the latter, for they trampled the White House nurseries, gardens, even the trees he had planted for posterity. He was similarly thwarted in the end with his other great botanical endeavor of providing the American navy with an assured supply of live oak for ship construction.

He was more fortunate with his gardens in Quincy; there he suffered only the usual defeats common to all who toil in the ground. Small though they were, they kept him happily occupied as he advanced in years. Every time he looked at the "shellbark walnut" in his garden and the Mazzard cherry north of his house, both of which he had planted in 1804, he was reminded of how much he had learned about plants. At age sixty-six he was still "plucking up weeds—a never ceasing occupation" that he probably pursued until his death at age eighty-one. He died on the floor of the House of Representatives in 1848.

Andrew Jackson

1 8 2 9 - 3 7

Andrew Jackson could not have come upon the scene as an American farmer at a better time and place. Born some twenty-four years after Thomas Jefferson, with the Revolutionary War behind the country, Jackson was free as a young man to move west from the border of North and South Carolina, the scene of his birth, to seek his fortune, following the example of other adventurous young men. The loss of his father just prior to his birth in 1767, followed by the death of his brother Hugh in 1780 and of his mother and his brother Robert in 1781 might have overwhelmed a less stalwart youngster. Such a calamity was compensated somewhat by the fact that Andrew now held clear ownership of his father's 200-acre farm, deeded to him and his brothers by his mother in 1770. His Irish grandfather Hugh Jackson left him a legacy of 300 or 400 pounds sterling in 1783, which could have eased his way still further except for the fact that Jackson soon lost this sizable stake as the result of his gambling on horseraces and cockfights. (He was to do better with his father's land, selling it in 1793.)

By 1780, at age thirteen, Jackson had joined a unit of dragoons on the American side of the Revolutionary War and was made a mounted orderly and messenger. By the time he was seventeen he was teaching in the Waxhaw settlement and then after reading law was admitted to the North Carolina bar in 1787. Jackson was off and running and never looked back.

He decided that his career would best be advanced in the western district of North Carolina, later to become the state of Tennessee. His relocation was timely, and his training as a lawyer immediately stood him in good stead. He became the attorney general (i.e., the public prosecutor) of the region. The first permanent settlement in the area was near Knoxville; the year, 1756. After several false starts beginning in 1785, Tennessee finally became a state in 1796. Jackson's arrival in 1788 and his visible public job thus made it possible for him to become influential at an early age in the politics of his chosen home. He helped frame the Tennessee constitution and was elected the state's first congressman in 1796 and a senator in 1797. He became a justice of Tennessee's supreme court in 1798, leaving the bench six years later. In the following decades Jackson served his country in a variety of other capacities, military and political, culminating this facet of his life by serving as president of the United States from 1829 to 1837.

But Andrew Jackson had another occupation: farmer. His father had been a farmer in the Waxhaw area before his death. His mother's kin, who lived in the region and with whom Andrew's mother lived with her boys after her husband's death, also followed that line of work, but young Jackson was too much the rambunctious youth to work the fields. Besides, the Revolutionary War had been fought on home territory, and Andrew was caught up in the excitement and danger of that ongoing affair. Since the age of thirteen he had demonstrated a willingness to take chances, even to risk his life. Later he would not be daunted by the thought of running a plantation with no practical experience to guide him or knowledge gained from books. It was just one more instance of Andrew Jackson's living by his wits.

Whatever evaluation one may have of his political abilities and legacy, all must agree that this man was an unqualified success as a planter, although he was apparently unmindful that even the soils of Tennessee could eventually become exhausted. Records of those who called at his home, The Hermitage, attest to his reputation as a progressive farmer. For example, the former governor of Tennessee William Blount commented after his visit in 1824 that the land was, as he expressed it, very fertile and beautiful and handsomely arranged. Blount was impressed with the size of the fields and their clear cultivation. Jackson's meadows and pastures, said he, were similarly large and well kept. He also commented that the plantation horses, cattle, hogs, and sheep were of the best breeds and in excellent condition.

Jackson's management skills were his forte and made it possible for him to succeed when others failed. In this, like John Adams before him, Jackson had an irreplaceable asset: Rachel, a wife interested in agriculture and horticulture. Frontier women were valued for their fortitude, intelligence, and independent ways, provided that their husbands had enough self-confidence not to worry that their wives might learn to manage without them. No one ever accused Andrew of a lack of self-confidence, and no one ever accused Rachel of not thoroughly knowing the intricacies of plantation management.

Although Andrew no doubt set down general goals to be achieved concerning the fields and stock (he, after all, was the one responsible for the family finances), there were periods of time, especially during his active military career, when Rachel made do alone. In addition to the field work, her responsibilities also included getting sheep shorn, clothing and shoes made, and the multitude of other activities involved with running what was in effect a small town. Jackson was free with his praise of her performance. Like most plantation owners he found knowledgeable, dependable overseers virtually impossible to find.

His other ace was his yearly practice at the first of January to add up what he owed, pay his bills at once, and apportion the rest of his cash to the remaining months. At the end even this measure did not save him, but his problems, as we shall see, stemmed from a profligate adopted son, not his own want of expertise.

The crop he chose to grow, cotton, had been cultivated in this country for domestic use since colonial times. Separating the seed from the lint of the green-seed, short-staple variety suitable for the soil and climate in upland regions, however, was a distinct handicap for a plant that otherwise could be so useful. Sea-island cotton, introduced in 1786, solved this difficulty, but it could be grown successfully only in the lowlands along the southeastern coast, where human disease was prevalent. Eli Whitney and his invention of the cotton gin in 1793 made possible large-scale commerical production of the variety most easily exploited. He thereby changed southern agriculture and American history as well.

Short-staple cotton became the largest commercial crop in

the south, the basis not only of its economy but also of its social life. The means to capitalize on the new machine were all in place. Slavery was an established institution. Lands amendable to cotton culture were cheap, plentiful, and undiminished in their fertility. The culture of cotton was well known and was not difficult. Jackson took full advantage of the circumstances. U.S. exports increased from 275 bales of cotton in 1797 to 36,000 in 1800, indicating how quickly prospects for the south had changed.

Just when or how Jackson decided to become a farmer is not clear. Like most other cotton planters, farming was for him a method of making money; he does not seem to have had a love for the land for its other values, as Jefferson, for example, did. In 1800 an estimated 90 percent of the American population engaged in that occupation with most of the remainder nonetheless growing part of their food supply. Jackson himself was only twenty-one when he arrived in what later became Tennessee. He knew he would have to earn some money before he could become a land holder of any consequence. This he accomplished with his job as attorney general to the extent that he managed to acquire acreage thirty miles north of the settlement of Natchez, where he established a trading store. In 1791 he married Rachel Donelson, and in the following year he bought a 330-acre tract on the Cumberland River, where the two established their first home. By 1795 Jackson had purchased Hunter's Hill outside of Nashville, a finer plantation still. He would later buy property elsewhere, but he seems to have decided very early that Nashville would be his home.

With his star rising in Tennessee, Jackson built a handsome house in the expectation that his farming and the trading store he established at Hunter's Hill would justify it. By 1798 Hunter's

Hill showed a profit, a good indication of his ability to learn quickly the intricacies involved in plantation ownership. He added a distillery to his plantation equipment and purchased a cotton gin, becoming one of the first in his part of the state to own one. With his own private landing and ferry, he must have felt that his future was secure and finally centered on one spot, unlike the life of wandering that had preceded his marriage. This was not to be. Hunter's Hill was sold in 1804 to raise cash to meet his obligations, which had been exacerbated by a raging financial panic and misplaced confidence in a wealthy Philadelphia man whose notes Jackson had accepted and endorsed.

Fortunately for him in 1795 he had also purchased at The Hermitage 640 acres of fertile rolling land that was adjacent to Hunter's Hill, with still another adjoining tract of 640 acres added the following year. (The latter property was sold with Hunter's Hill.) The Hermitage had been built as a block house some time prior to Jackson's purchase. This he remodeled, and it served as his residence from 1804 until a second home, also called The Hermitage, was built in 1818 in a secluded meadow selected by Rachel. This house, extensively remodeled in 1831, was destroyed by fire in 1834 and rebuilt the following year.

Although farm matters naturally consumed much of Jackson's interest in this period, he was determined to beautify The Hermitage beyond the 1,000 peach and apple trees he had planted in 1801. Orchards were a common feature of American farms, although the Jacksons' was larger than most. Jackson no doubt planted the trees with an eye to selling the resulting cider and peach brandy at his store. As apple varieties of the era were not well suited to central Tennessee, the cider scheme may have been ill considered, with Jackson reduced to appreciating the floral display in spring. This was ample recompense, no doubt, as Jackson had a love of flowers.

He also had in mind a grander plan for which, in 1819, he hired William Frost, a "regular bred english Gardener," to landscape the grounds. Jackson's spelling and grammar were not polished, but he knew what he wanted, and Frost had an excellent reputation in Philadelphia. The Jacksons had recently toured Mt. Vernon and viewed the gardens there with delight. Andrew wrote a charming description of what they had seen, leaving no doubt that he very much appreciated the flowering plants and understood the pleasure they could bring to one's life.

The landscaping plan that evolved was worthy of the house he had built for Rachel. A beautiful lawn shaded by mature forest trees was approached through a coppice of oak, hickory, and sycamore to the brick gate posts flanking the bowed drive, bordered by young cedars from the nearby woods, which led to the house. Adjacent to the house was a fenced acre, with appropriate gate, that was devoted to flowers. The area was circled and bisected by gravel walks edged with bricks especially made on the plantation for that purpose. Jackson often wrote about this garden, favoring, tradition says, the pinks and roses. While Rachel was alive she took charge of it. After her death her husband was hard put to find overseers who paid proper attention to its appearance. He had sent seeds from Washington and Philadelphia to fill the beds, and Rachel had gone beyond the garden area to bring in wildflowers that caught her fancy. These all had to be protected to preserve her memory and his equanimity.

A woman who visited The Hermitage while Jackson but not Rachel still lived remembered years later the herbs edging the flower beds, the bulbs, and the variety of rosebushes among the plants in this Tennessee garden and wrote a glowing account of it all.

Because of his beautification of The Hermitage, Jackson was well disposed to do the same for the President's Park. Like John Quincy Adams before him, he found solace in this outdoor occupation when things were going wrong at the office; Jackson had never been happy as a legislator. Just as he had relied on someone else to lay out the grounds at his own home, he seems to have been content to follow the plans laid out by Jefferson and Latrobe as transmuted through the minds of Monroe's Bulfinch, and then John Quincy. There is at least no indication that anyone else made an attempt to change the broad outlines devised so many years before.

Considering Jackson's interest in such matters, what is more surprising is that serious work on landscaping did not begin until his second term in the spring of 1833. Perhaps grief over his beloved wife's death just prior to his taking office continued to haunt and thereby incapacitate him. Given their common enjoyment of the garden, perhaps Jackson could not bring himself to consider landscaping the White House grounds so soon after this unfortunate event. He was also incapacitated by his own poor health, which plagued him throughout his presidency. Perhaps he recognized the prior necessity of bringing running water into the house, a plan for which now existed; or, as an avid horseman with fine horses needing better accommodations, he saw a greater need of building a new stable so he could keep up this form of active exercise.

But for one used to beauty around his house in the form of landscaping that included flowers his own dear wife had so assiduously attended, the planting extravaganza at the White

House that occurred during Jackson's second term must have been the direct result of his encouragement. After all, some succeeding presidents gave no encouragement at all, and consequently little if anything was changed on the grounds on their watch. As for Andrew Jackson, the man and the very apparent need to civilize finally the bare ground around the great house met. The Park under Jackson came of age, indicating to all who saw it that this anchor of Pennsylvania Avenue was fashionable too.

Washington was ready now for these improvements after some thirty years of growing pains. The *National Intelligencer*, the newspaper of Jefferson and Madison's old friends Samuel Harrison Smith and his wife, Margaret Bayard Smith, provided suggestions as to how the grounds might be improved, as did other newspapers in the early 1830s. Adequate financing remained a problem, but at least the public in general seems to have perceived the need to tidy up what was really an eyesore.

Because of its extensiveness, beautification lasted several years. Beginning in the summer of 1833, work was done on all fronts. The initial emphasis was on additional grading. In an age of hand labor, progress was slow, even though many men were employed—more than sixty in this period. The ground was loosened with hoes, shovels, even oxen and plows, with excess dirt carried around or away by wheelbarrows and draymen's carts and the remainder raked smooth.

Against this background, new features took their place. In the summer of 1833 work began on the north fence. Jackson was unhappy with the curving structure built along Pennsylvania Avenue by Monroe as well as with the placement of the gates and piers he had had constructed. The new president ordered the

Fence at north front as changed by A. Jackson. Note North Portico, built in 1829–30, and new iron railing adjacent to the façade. (Library of Congress)

north curve made straight and the gates and piers moved farther apart. Parallel to the north façade a low parapet with an elaborate iron railing for the first time gave protection from the deep areaway along the building. It also finished off the new look of the front of the house, which now sported a portico, finally completed in 1830. The wall was extended on each side of the front lawn to connect the front and back. Jackson took sufficient interest in it to make changes personally, effectively doubling the original cost. Despite the fact that the appropriation ran out, the fence was completed for fear that Washington's still-wandering cattle would penetrate the lawn area. It remained in place until Theodore Roosevelt's term (1901–09), when it was replaced by a solid parapet.

By May of the following year grading was far enough along so that the driveway, remodeled into a wide horseshoe shape, could be moved to its present location, graveled and edged with paved walks. The ironwork on the walls was painted black, and the piers of the gates as well as the base of the walls were painted white to match the house. Some minor grading to improve drainage was undertaken later, but the area was now essentially completed. It was planted with grass, and sheep were counted on to keep it cut.

Cows, housed in the west wing and later nearby, kept the grass down south of the wall. The boxes were removed from the few trees John Quincy had planted that had prospered and gotten large enough to avoid damage by the sheep. The front of the mansion could now be viewed by one and all with pride.

The south lawn area received even more attention. Its potential had perhaps been realized only by Jefferson, if only in his mind's eye. The reality was still quite grim except for the fact that trees planted for screening off the house from the Capitol axis of Pennsylvania Avenue had grown sufficiently to do their job. Basic to the undertaking was the need for further grading, which was done. The colonnades on either side of the house were hidden by newly created slopes to screen off the domestic tasks accomplished there during the warmest part of the year. The South Portico, completed in 1824, would now be set off to advantage with a proper lawn. The road Jefferson had laid out was leveled, with gravel added to its surface to provide easier access. His stone wall, although crumbling in places, still marked this border of the south lawn. Beyond that the ground to the river remained in its natural state.

Of perhaps greater importance to Jackson were the gardens devoted to flowers. The impetus to grow them certainly did not come from the surrounding community, where people devoted their energies to raising fruits and vegetables. Jackson had an ally in John Ousley, the gardener first hired by John Quincy, whose forte was attention to detail. Flower growing is a fussy occupation, and Ousley found pleasure in making cuttings and setting out plants. The two-acre fenced flower garden southeast of the house remained his to command, to plant, to weed, and to oversee the raking of the gravel paths and trimming the grass borders. Roses

French-style parterres on south grounds, 1831. The South Portico was added in 1824. (Library of Congress)

were, of course, prominent, with dwarf rose trees first used in Jackson's time. Ousley also tended spring bulbs of various sorts, flowering shrubs like the single and double altheas John Quincy had enjoyed, camellias, and flowering trees. In other words, Ousley was responsible for the maintenance of the grounds. The result must surely have been pleasing.

A second man, William Whelan, was hired to concentrate on growing vegetables. Like gardeners elsewhere, he was expected to save seeds and know how to start those requiring it in cold frames, glass bell jars, and clay pots in sunny windows. His domain, also fenced, was southwest of the house. The division indicates that growing flowers and vegetables was upgraded to a more serious level.

A third man, Jemmy Maher, completed the crew. Maher was

in reality the city's public gardener, who was pressed into service for the president's landscaping projects. Having been appointed by Jackson to his post, Maher had a special reason to pursue the president's plan. Maher's position and responsibilities were quite different from those of the other two men. He owned a nursery in town that provided him with numerous contacts advantageous to his benefactor's scheme. He was used to securing laborers (from Ireland) and planning and supervising large numbers at work. He knew the nurseries from which he could secure the plant material he wanted. He bought mainly from William Prince and Sons and Bloodgood & Co., both of Long Island, by then the largest and most national of the nation's horticultural establishments. Maher could fully understand too the financial advantages of buying plants at estate sales. In fact, as public gardener he could freely tap some of those funds for the White House. Couple these assets with the ability to think big and work for an employer who was enthusiastic about the outcome, and progress can be extraordinary.

Maher ordered numerous trees for the White House grounds—horse chestnuts with their beautiful flowers, sycamores with their interesting bark patterns, graceful elms, and sturdy maples. The magnolias attributed to Jackson would have been planted at this time. The Lombardy poplars Jefferson had planted on Pennsylvania Avenue were replaced, as the third president had well understood these short-lived but fast-growing trees would be. However, Maher used elms instead of the willow oaks that Margaret Bayard Smith wrote Jefferson had intended. Now, even though the elms were small, the avenue did not present a barren appearance if only because a forty-five-foot-wide strip in the center was paved. Washington was no longer a raw frontier town.

Maher was apparently involved with Ousley's flowers to the extent of overseeing construction of an arbor, numerous trellises, fences, and garden benches. He was probably also involved with the construction of Jackson's orangery. This was based on the shell of a fireproof vault, an appendage of the old Treasury Building that had been abandoned after the burning of Washington by the British. It was connected to the east side of the mansion by a low brick wall that because of the slope of the site had concealed the working areas of the house from Pennsylvania Avenue. Unfortunately the orangery required constant care. It is thought to have housed, among other plants, a sago palm rescued from George Washington's orangery, which burned in 1835. As the south grounds were not open to the public, details of how it appeared are virtually confined to bills incurred. The fact that

Lithograph by D. W. Kellog & Co., 183-? (Library of Congress)

these gardens were held solely for the use and enjoyment of the president and those invited by him, to the exclusion of others except members of Congress, indicates how much they meant to Jackson: His motive in creating them was not to impress anyone but to fulfill a deep-seated need of his own.

All the while he was president, Jackson, like his predecessors, could not afford to forget his plantation. When he left The Hermitage for Washington he put farm management into the hands of his and Rachel's adopted son Andrew Jackson Jr. This boy was one of several the childless Jacksons reared as their own. Just out of his teens, Jackson Jr. would not become involved in politics if his father could help it. By 1832 the son married. The older man then wrote a compact manual on plantation management at The Hermitage to provide needed guidance. The senior Jackson was used to giving the management of his property to others. Indeed, he could not do otherwise as he served his country in various political and military posts. Heretofore he could and did count on Rachel to supervise the family fortunes. Between his keen eye for what needed to be done and her ability to see it executed they were a resounding success. Now Rachel was dead. It was not surprising that her widower would choose their son to follow in her footsteps.

Regretably, Jackson Jr. was slow to catch on as to what was expected of him. At least this was the view that his father took. It is always difficult for a parent to come to grips with a child's failings. The young man seems to have lacked not intelligence as much as character, despite his upbringing. He was to prove a constant trial throughout the remainder of his father's life. Yet his parent remained sanguine.

At this time Hunter's Hill, which Jackson had been forced to sell earlier, was now back on the market. Its 563 acres adjoined The Hermitage, which would keep his namesake close by. In 1833 negotiations for its purchase were begun. Jackson Jr.'s character flaws now became more firmly entrenched—and evident. His father found that the younger man was not reporting honestly or expeditiously on his debts, how much cotton was being taken to market, and how much money it brought. Yet Jackson pursued the plan of buying back Hunter's Hill. His dreams for this son refused to die despite the evidence of the latter's inadequacies. As Jackson saw it, his boy did not yet understand the instructions for plantation management he had been given earlier, so he wrote a second set, detailing every component. Economy, he stressed, was the key to remaining solvent.

In addition to these revelations of his son's apparent inability to handle money and details, Jackson was struck another blow at home when The Hermitage burned on October 13, 1834. It was unthinkable not to restore the home that meant so much to him, and so it was rebuilt. This cost, added to what was still owed on the purchase of Hunter's Hill, must have caused the president some anxious moments. He took refuge in Ousley's gardens on the south lawn of the White House whenever he was in Washington.

In this period Jackson was also rethinking the very basis of his agriculture, in reality of all agriculture in the Cumberland Valley. Heretofore he had concentrated on cotton, as did other farmers in Davidson County. Cotton had two drawbacks. First, the growing season was not really long enough. Second, prices fluctuated too much to make it a reliable cash crop, although

Jackson's cotton had a reputation for being of the best, and consequently he got top dollar. Now he thought it would be wiser to diversify, to include hemp and perhaps some tobacco along with livestock, not only for himself but for his neighbors as well. He set his new plans in motion.

Thus on a number of fronts Jackson could hardly wait for his second term to end. He had become a tired old man who wanted the peace and quiet of The Hermitage, which had always rejuvenated him. What he found upon his arrival would have destroyed a lesser man. The new roof on the rebuilt house was leaking, the livestock had not been fed properly, supplies for the year had not been bought. To solve his financial problems Jackson did what he had done before to avoid going into debt: He sold land, this time acreage in western Tennessee he had bought in more affluent days when he, along with many others, engaged in land speculation.

With renewed vigor now that he was home, he personally supervised The Hermitage. Results were immediately good. Despite this, Jackson was brought to financial destitution because of his son's continued irresponsibility. Stalwart friends assumed the continuing losses, thereby saving the old man. This happy condition did not last because of his continued inability to face his namesake's limitations. Yet throughout the years the General had himself been loyal to his land. When the results of the 1824 presidential election became known, giving John Quincy that post, Jackson, whose name had been put into contention, said with conviction, "How often does my thoughts lead me back to the Hermitage, there surrounded by a few friends would be a paradise. . . ."[1] In 1833, at the beginning of his own second term in the highest office in the land, he said with equal conviction, "I long for retirement & respose on the Hermitage."[2] And at the end of his eight years he expressed his relief: "I hope rest in due time may restore my health so as to be enabled to amuse myself in riding over my farm and visiting my neighbors."[3]

Martin Van Buren

1 8 3 7 - 4 1

After the Jackson years there was little left on the White House grounds for his immediate successor to do in terms of additional beautification. This was just as well. Martin Van Buren, who followed Jackson in office, was never a hands-on gardener. Nonetheless he was most appreciative of the finer things in life. As his estate, Lindenwald, would later demonstrate, he had a keen eye for good landscaping.

The son of a farmer and tavern keeper, as a youth Van Buren had done his part in the fields with his eight brothers and sisters, but his quick mind saw money-making possibilities in the law. Never again, it appears, did he get his hands dirty by farming or gardening. Neither stirred his soul as politics did. This is evident when one considers that despite his obvious abilities and relative wealth, not until his retirement from the presidency did he buy a home as a permanent residence.

Although he had bought a house in Hudson, New York, after his marriage in 1807, it was clear that the ambitious young man would soon move on to bigger and better jobs in other places. He had also owned farms and several farm houses in Kinderhook, his birthplace, and in surrounding New York towns along the Hudson River. Yet he spent virtually all of his adult life until his retirement in boarding or rented houses, rented rooms or hotels, any living quarters other than his own. His wife had died when he was thirty-seven after bearing him four sons. An all-male household could get by with these arrangements. His frequent and lengthy tours on legal and political business, upon which he throve, were not conducive to the establishment of a home.

One of his absences occurred after Van Buren resigned as secretary of state in Jackson's cabinet upon his appointment by the president in 1831 to become the American minister to England. Although he was not confirmed to the post, while there he toured English estates, recording his observations as Jefferson had done more than fifty years before. With this recent experience behind him he may have served as a sounding board for White House improvements upon his return, when he became vice president in Jackson's second term. He certainly would look with approval at the efforts of the outdoor crews and lend his support to the extent that he could. This would be contribution enough, considering the political blast that was to come.

During Van Buren's single term as president, management of the White House grounds remained the domain of John Ousley, William Whelan, and Jemmy Maher as before. Additional potted fruit trees were added to the orangery. The lawn was still watered by a small piece of equipment, bought in Jackson's term, that operated on the same principle as that of a fire engine. It consisted of a large wooden vat on wheels filled with water and rolled to wherever it was needed. Van Buren, ever mindful of appearances, added circular iron benches around some of the larger trees and, for the flower garden, cast-iron chairs and benches.

Van Buren must have been constrained in doing more by the speech of Congressman Charles Ogle of Pennsylvania on April 14, 1840 (and two days thereafter), midway through Van Buren's term. Ogle's theme was what he called the wasteful expenditure of money by Congress to make the White House "a royal establishment." The speech was then published and liberally distributed to advance its goal, which was to ridicule Van Buren.[1] It had been prompted by the president's audacious request for $3,665 for alterations and repairs plus furniture for the interior and for the exterior, additional trees, shrubs, compost, and superintendence of the grounds. President Martin Van Buren, claimed the congressman, was responsible for such unwarranted ostentation as could be seen at the White House.

Ogle detailed this horrendous state of affairs to his fellow lawmakers, positively wallowing in the inappropriateness of the "choice collection of both native plants and exotics" both outdoors and in the orangery, all the result of the hard-working Ousely, Whelan, and Maher. Now that the trees and shrubs were at or approaching maturity, the grounds at last must have given the appearance of modest elegance, although they could hardly have rivaled the long-established lavish gardens of European kings and nobility. Ogle's exasperation was probably due more to the fact Van Buren carried on Andrew Jackson's practice of keeping the south grounds free of public use.

The president, said Ogle, was overpaid at $25,000 a year, certainly a large sum compared with the incomes of most Americans. The president, he maintained, should use his own money to beautify the grounds of the mansion he was privileged to occupy. Ogle provided the specifics of what Congress had already spent to glorify its chief executive. Ten acts of Congress between 1829 and 1839 had provided more than enough. As the records do not specify whether the sums Ogle quoted were spent indoors or out, it is somewhat difficult to tell whether those for the outdoors were justified.

Nevertheless, Ogle railed against the total: $88,722.58, most of it spent in the Jackson years. He gasped at the total cost of building and rebuilding the White House in 1814, plus the development of the grounds: $634,703.25 for the mansion alone. He got a lot of mileage out of this significant amount, although he neglected to acknowledge the size of both the mansion and the President's Park and the hard use both were subjected to by the public and in the public interest. He was obviously not concerned with the image projected to foreign envoys used to more dazzling government centers. As for him, he thought the state of the house and grounds at the end of John Quincy's administration sufficient for the "taste and judgement of our plain, republican farmers." Ogle died a year later, but the results of his bombast lingered on.

Although Van Buren sought a second term (which he was denied), he had already prepared for his retirement midway through his first term by buying the old William P. Van Ness home one mile southeast of the center of Kinderhook. The Van Nesses, distant relatives of his, represented the well-to-do side of the extended Van Buren family. Their house was well suited for the type of permanent residence the president had in mind. The lindens, notable among the lawn trees, supplied Van Buren with the name he chose for his estate: Lindenwald.

The house and the 50 acres that came with it were supplemented by Van Buren with an adjoining 150 acres. His first projects upon leaving Washington in March 1841 were to restore both house and grounds, too long neglected. The lawn was plowed up, fertilized, seeded, and rolled. Crumbling stone walls and rotting stiles were repaired or replaced, as were the outbuildings. Part of a cornfield nearby was transformed into a kitchen garden. Van Buren may not have actively farmed or gardened since childhood, but he was a quick study. His character traits and managerial skills, honed by years in a successful career in law and politics, were equally applicable to running a northern farm. His practical good sense and his enjoyment of hard work, upon which he throve, coupled with a judicious expenditure of his rather considerable means brought quick—and lasting—results to satisfy any farmer. Although his land had been under cultivation for 160 years and rented for 20, the fields of this Hudson River countryside had remained rich.

At the end of the first year home he was able to report to Andrew Jackson on his good fortune in both the kitchen garden and the ornamental grounds. "Everybody that sees it," Van Buren told his old White House mate, "says that I have made one of the finest places in the state."[2]

The farm acreage was similarly quickly made productive with the help of Martin Jr. and a "Mr. Marquette." Son Smith shared his father's interests and pride in the family estate, and he too would direct the farm in the elder Van Buren's absence. With good land and able management, Van Buren within short order had ample fruit, vegetables, poultry, pork, beef, mutton, and dairy products for his own use and could offer hay, oats, and potatoes for sale. In 1842 he declared a profit of $700 on his apples and pears.

Although he had been paid $25,000 a year as president, his income afterward was only between $5,000 and $7,000 from money lent on good security. But neither were his expenses as great as they had been in his presidential years, although family members and guests were common at his table. He was long accustomed to budgeting closely, and lived out his life in comfortable circumstances.

Interim

1841-50

After the presidency of Martin Van Buren, little was done about the White House grounds for the next decade. His successor, William Henry Harrison, died of pneumonia after only thirty days in office. John Tyler, who then assumed the post, had a stormy presidency, and unlike some of his predecessors, he apparently found no solace in the garden. James Polk followed in Tyler's footsteps, both in service in office and his lack of compulsion to change anything on the grounds. The Polks were more interested in revamping the interior of the great house, which had been left to deteriorate since Andrew Jackson's occupancy.

The only major outdoor job begun during Polk's administration (1845–49) was undertaken not for purposes of beautification but to preserve the presidential health. South of the mansion off toward the river the land was so low that it invited the onslaught of malaria and cholera. The Commissioner of Public Buildings,

Drawing by August Köllner, 1848. (Library of Congress)

123

Charles Douglas, initiated in 1848 a plan to eliminate the much-feared diseases. Perhaps taking the idea from Pierre Charles L'Enfant's of the preceding century, Douglas proposed to grade the slope south of the house into terraces and plant them with trees and shrubs. Congress appropriated the money, and work was begun at once.

The lack of good drainage was exacerbated by Tiber Creek. Its origin was to the northeast of the White House, and it overflowed at high tide onto the Mall. To overcome the problem, a canal was eventually built in part of the creek bed. But this had proved to be only partially successful and with its own pollution in fact increased the potential for disease. The city's generally primitive water and sanitation system did not help matters. Not until the Grant administration (1869–77) was a program initiated to transform the city into a modern one in this and other regards. Polk himself died a few months after leaving the White House, and his death was widely attributed to the unhealthful vapors surrounding the mansion.

Zachary Taylor (1849–50), who followed Polk in office, probably died of cholera. Millard Fillmore, who followed Taylor, was spared, but his successor, Franklin Pierce, came down with malaria during his term (and survived it). No wonder presidents had been prone to leave Washington during the warmest months.

Interestingly, Taylor shared much of Fillmore's background but did nothing about the White House grounds (and apparently made no important changes to the mansion itself). Perhaps this can be attributed to the fact he died unexpectedly after only a year and a half as president. Taylor, like Fillmore, had been a surveyor in his youth. The fathers of both men had been farmers, and both presidents had learned farming in their youth. Taylor expanded on this early experience by becoming a farmer himself, much in the mode of the earliest presidents. Like them, he saw the desirability of soil conservation and crop rotation beyond his cotton staple. He experimented not only with different strains of cotton but also with crops of tobacco, corn, wheat, peas, and hay. His were largely self-sufficient lands, with sheep, cattle, hogs, and poultry.

Taylor began his career as a farmer with a wedding gift of 324 acres of land in what is now downtown Louisville, Kentucky. In the following years he became preoccupied with land speculation, but his home was the 1,923-acre Cypress Grove Plantation on the Mississippi River north of Natchez. In 1848, shortly before he became president, Taylor wrote, "The subject of farming is one to which I have devoted much of my life, and in which I yet continue to take the deepest interest."[1] His intellectual thrusts in fact were confined to agriculture and how the various facets of it would affect his plantations.

Meanwhile, during Polk's and Taylor's tenures the President's Park was still under the experienced and capable hands of John Ousley and Jemmy Maher. (William Whalen was no longer working as the kitchen gardener by the time Polk arrived.) The two men continued the landscaping plans set forth under Andrew Jackson. Maher, the more enterprising, had his own nursery business to supplement his government income. This relegated Ousley to the role of secondary player in maintaining the grounds. Even had either been inclined to do more, a tight budget provided by the Congress would have prevented any new major project. Ousley in effect was a general maintenance man, taking care of his flowers, vegetables, orangery, and lawn, providing the residents of the great house with food and visual enjoyment when it was wanted. The extent of his additional enterprise during this period was confined to selling lawn grass to a livery stable owner, whose employees cut it for hay. A farmer was then allowed to graze his sheep, again for a fee. With the money he received, Ousley bought gardening tools and supplies.

The overall design Maher had labored to produce was now evident. Shrubs were grouped, which made them easier to water and to fence against wandering sheep and horses. Trees, still on the small side and not too many, nonetheless helped provide the proper setting for the kind of small focal points of beauty Jefferson had so much appreciated. Flowers, particularly roses, played their part but never in competition with the house itself or the expanses of lawn. All this would change radically under the vision of another landscaper, Andrew Jackson Downing, under the benevolent eyes of President Millard Fillmore.

Millard Fillmore

1 8 5 0 - 5 3

Millard Fillmore was the right man in the right place for the next big push to landscape the public grounds in Washington. When dealing with an area as large as that which surrounded the White House and extended to the Capitol (i.e., the Mall), special skills above and beyond a love of gardening, which Fillmore and his wife shared, were almost essential. These skills involved surveying and map reading. In both of these Fillmore was proficient. He could discern good draftsmanship when he saw it, and his love of maps caused him to bring his collection to the White House. Fillmore's use of his presidential time in working with Andrew Jackson Downing may well have been spurred by a need to escape the unresolvable political situation in the decade preceding the Civil War.

Fillmore, like John Tyler, became president upon the death of his predecessor, in his case, the enormously popular Zachary

Taylor. With only 2 years and 237 days as president, Fillmore may not have left his stamp on the political scene, but in his innovations to the public grounds he accomplished a great deal. As a vice president interested in city planning, he was ready to go into action as soon as he was sworn into office.

Ignatius Mudd had succeeded Charles Douglas as Commissioner of Public Buildings. Whereas Douglas in his brief tenure had limited his activities in the area surrounding the White House to the development of terraces on the south lawn, Mudd, a Taylor appointee, took a broader view. Washington had continued to grow. Where other contemporaries had concentrated on ideas for the development of small segments of the public lands, Mudd decided upon a different route. An overall landscaping plan should be developed instead. Andrew Jackson Downing, acknowledged as the leading landscape gardener in America, was given the job with Fillmore's endorsement.

Congressman Charles Ogle's complaints during Martin Van Buren's tenure were once more about to be heard. He had protested that in 1825 under John Quincy Adams $5,000 had been appropriated for leveling, grading, "&c." the President's Park and that John Quincy

took measures to carry into effect the intention of Congress by digging down the knolls, and by filling up the hollows, and in this manner levelling or making plain and flat the surface of the ground. But . . . "variety is the very spice of life" and so thought our reformers [i.e., Van Buren]. The survey of smooth lawns and gently sloping meads covered with rich coats of white and red clover, and luxuriant grass, make no delightful impression on their eyes. [For Van Buren] mere meadows are too common to gratify the refined taste of an exquisite with "sweet sandy whiskers." He must have undulations, "beautiful mounds, and other contrivances" to ravish his exalted and etherel soul. Hence the reformers have constructed a number of clever sized hills, every pair of which it is said, was designed to resemble and assume the form of AN AMAZON'S BOSOM, with a miniature knoll or hillock on its apex, to denote the n-pple. Thousands of the People's dollars have been thrown away on these silly fancies, which are better adapted to please the sickly and vicious tastes of palace dandies, than to gratify the simple eye of plain, republican freemen.[1]

One must wonder what Ogle would have thought of Downing's plan.

Only the impossibility of achieving the sheer scope of Downing's vision with the money Congress was likely to appropriate prevented a total upheaval in the public domain. Downing made his mark instead on the area south of the mansion and on the Mall, that grassy stretch between the White House and the Capitol. The former required a master hand to solve the drainage problems it presented, while the latter needed a master hand to coordinate the various parts into a unified whole. Downing had what it took to tackle the job. His age, a mere thirty-three at the time he accepted the assignment, probably caused some resentment among his elders. Nevertheless, something of a consensus had been reached by Washington officialdom that a master plan was needed. Furthermore, landscape architecture was a profession still new to America. There were not many candidates from whom to choose.

Downing's father owned on the Hudson River a nursery that the son soon enlarged to his benefit. His precocity was evident. In 1841 at the tender age of twenty-six the younger Downing had published his first book, *The Theory and Practice of Landscape*

Gardening, Adapted to North America, which made its appearance in the best libraries. This was followed by other tomes that established his reputation far beyond his nursery. His magazine *The Horticulturist*, which he edited, capped his burgeoning career.

By the fall of 1850, when he went to Washington, Downing can be forgiven for thinking he had the world by the tail. This assurance was reinforced by the fact that President Fillmore consistently took Downing's side whenever disputes arose. Downing in turn respected his president's expertise and sought his and Mrs. Fillmore's suggestions for the White House grounds—suggestions that the architect probably incorporated into his plans, as Benjamin Latrobe had done years earlier with Jefferson's.

Rural Architect, the title Downing insisted upon (as opposed to Public Gardener), indicated both that he expected to be treated as the professional he was and that he intended to emulate the English romantic style rather than the earlier formal landscapes. These were his goals:

> 1st: To form a national Park which should be an ornament to the Capital of the United States: 2nd: To give an example of the natural style of Landscape Gardening which may have an influence on the general taste of the Country: 3rd To form a collection of all the trees that will grow in the climate of Washington, and, by having these trees plainly labelled with their popular and scientific names, to form a public museum of living trees and shrubs where every person visiting Washington could become familiar with the habits and growth of all the hardy trees.[2]

Having made notes and gathered together the pertinent topographical maps the preceding autumn, Downing was ready

To His Excellency
The President of the
United States.

(A Copy.)

Explanatory Notes:

To accompany the plan for improving the Public Grounds at Washington.

My object in this Plan has been three fold: 1st To form a national Park, which should be an ornament to the Capital of the United States: 2nd To give an example of the natural style of Landscape Gardening which may have an influence on the general taste of the Country; 3rd To form a collection of all the trees that will grow in the climate of Washington, and, by having these trees plainly labelled with their popular and scientific names, to form a public museum of living trees and shrubs where every person visiting Washington could become familiar with the habits and growth of all the hardy trees.

The Public Grounds now to be improved, I have arranged so as to form six different and distinct scenes: viz: 1st

The President's Park or Parade. —

This comprises the open Ground directly south of the the President's House — Adopting suggestions made me at

A. J. Downing written plans for grounds and Mall, p. 1. (National Archives)

Washington I propose to keep the large area of this ground open, as a place for parade or military reviews, as well as public festivities or celebrations. A circular carriage-drive 40 feet wide, and nearly a mile long, shaded by an avenue of Elms, surrounds the Parade, while a series of foot-paths, 10 feet wide, winding through thickets of trees and shrubs, forms the boundary to this park, and would make an agreeable shaded promenade for pedestrians.—

I propose to take down the present small stone gates to the Presidents Grounds, and place at the end of Pennsylvania Avenue a large and handsome Archway of marble, which shall not only form the main entrance from the City to the whole of the proposed new Grounds, but shall also be one of the principal Architectural ornaments of

Presidents Arch
at the end of Penn.a Avenue.

the city; inside of this Arch-way is a semicircle with three gates commanding three carriage roads.—Two of these lead into the Parade or Presidents Park, the third is a private carriage-drive into the Presidents grounds; this gate should be protected by a Porters lodge, and should only be open on reception days,

A. J. Downing written plans for grounds and Mall, p. 2. (National Archives)

132

thus making the President's grounds on this side of the house quite private at all other times— I propose to have the <u>exit</u> of guests on reception days on this side of the house, the <u>entrance</u>, as now, on the other side. I have not shown on the plan several ideas that have occurred to me for increasing the beauty and seclusion of the President's grounds, because I would first wish to submit them for the approval of the President.

2nd. Monument Park.

This comprises the fine plot of ground surrounding the Washington monument and bordered by the Potomac. To reach it from the President's Park, I propose to cross the canal by a wire suspension bridge, sufficiently strong for carriages, which would permit vessels of moderate size to pass under it, and would be an <u>ornamental</u> feature in the grounds. I propose to plant Monument Park wholly with <u>American</u> trees, of large growth, disposed in open groups, so as to allow of fine vistas of the Potomac river.—

[Suspension bridge across the Canal]

A. J. Downing written plans for grounds and Mall, p. 3. (National Archives)

133

3rd. The Evergreen Garden.

Crossing 14th street * we next come to what I term the Evergreen Garden. This is a space of about 16 acres, laid out with walks so as to show every tree in detail, and planted wholly with evergreens. I propose to collect here all the evergreens, both foreign and native, that will thrive in the climate of Washington. At present, only about a dozen species of evergreen trees are known at Washington, but I will show that there are 130 species and varieties of fine evergreens which will thrive, in the open air, there. This includes not only the pine and fir tribe, with narrow leaves, but broad-leaved evergreens such as magnolias, Rhododendrons, Portugal laurels, &c. which, when assembled together in one place, would make such a winter garden scene as attractive, any pleasant day in mid-winter, as most gardens are in the midst of Summer. It would be a particularly valuable feature in Washington, where the Winter and early Spring months, are those in which the City has

---

* I propose finally, to have either hedges or light invisible iron fences to these streets, with gates at the crossings of the paths and carriage-drives - By arranging the planting as I have done, the streets would injure the general effect of the grounds as little as possible when the trees are well grown.

A. J. Downing written plans for grounds and Mall, p. 4. (National Archives)

by March 1851 to present them to Commissioner Ignatius Mudd. Congress, Charles Ogle notwithstanding, had done its part by appropriating money to begin work on the grounds south of the White House and on parts of the Mall.

Downing now revealed to one and all that Congressman Ogle had correctly assessed the propensities of most landscape architects: They would be swayed by what was currently popular and without a moment's hesitation obliterate what once had been considered quite stylish. L'Enfant had represented an older view, heavy on geometrical patterns. Unfortunately, from Downing's point of view, L'Enfant's plan established too many of the basic lines of the new District of Columbia, which by now were beyond changing. Jefferson and Latrobe were able to modify the ambience south of the White House within the stone wall, but even they had been unable to do anything about street alignment to the north, east, and west.

Downing's plan was most obviously fulfilled on the Mall (called by him the National Park). Just a field of grass, cows and sheep kept it mowed. As livestock are wont to do, they made clearly defined paths as they sought out especially tasty morsels. Downing proposed that the area be divided by thick groves of trees to break up its length. Footpaths and a road for carriages would follow the undulations of the natural terrain as they wound through the woods true to the romantic tradition of the Victorian age. Cognizant of the need for quick results, Downing proposed crosstrenching and fertilizing areas before they were planted with trees. Areas left to grass would provide a foil for the trees as well as vistas needed to provide variety. Horsedrawn mowers now used on English estates would keep the grass down. This would be a distinct change from John Ousley's use of scythes and sheep.

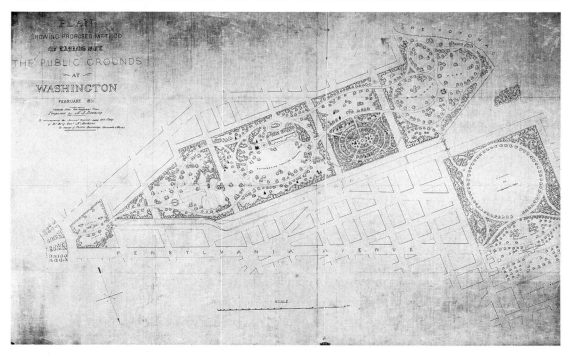

A. J. Downing plans for President's Park, 1851. (National Archives)

The National Park was adjacent to the White House grounds, where work was already in progress grading the land to the Tiber Creek. It was to be restyled now. (Indeed, the entire White House grounds were to be restyled.) In view of the new design, Downing designated this area to the south the "Parade" to distinguish it from the "President's Garden" immediately adjacent to the mansion. The Parade consisted of an enormous circle of grass surrounded by a forty-foot-wide, mile-long carriage drive lined with elms. Downing conceived it as the appropriate site "for parade or military reviews, as well as public festivities or celebrations." The whole was to be surrounded by groves of trees and shrubs through which ten-foot-wide footpaths wandered, making "an agreeable shaded promenade for pedestrians."

Downing's ideas for the Mall probably caused little flak.

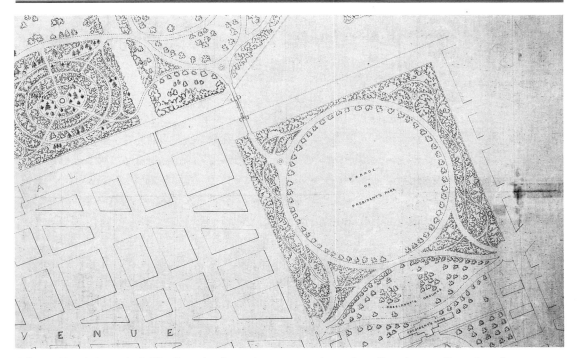

Downing plans: enlargement of Parade, 1851. (National Archives)

After all, although L'Enfant had made a tentative plan for the area, until now no one had seriously put forth any proposals as to what to do with it. Destroying what had already been built was something else. To make a unified whole of the expanse south of the White House, Jefferson's stone wall would have to be removed. This act could be more readily accepted, for the wall clearly interrupted the visual line and, furthermore, it was breaking down in places. (It was not demolished, though, until Grant's time.) Replacing Jefferson's venerated triple-arched brick gate at the east side of the grounds could cause a furor, although in the end it too was dismantled.

Downing had a more grandiose idea to solve the old problem of providing a suitable terminus to the west end of Pennsylvania Avenue. Like Jefferson, he would build an arch of triumph, this

137

one made of marble worthy of being "one of the principal Architectural ornaments of the city." Just inside the arch a semicircular court was laid out to direct traffic flow through either of two iron gates that led to the Parade or through the iron gate leading to the president's grounds. At the gate to the latter a guard would be stationed in a porter's lodge to control public access to the president's private yard, as Fillmore foresaw possible violence as the country drew nearer to a great sectional war. Now that the stone wall would be gone, Downing planned for an iron fence around the entire southern expanse with a minimal number of gates, all with suitable locks.

Access from the site of the new Washington Monument (begun in 1848 but not completed until thirty-four years later) on the Mall over Tiber Creek would be by a suspension bridge strong enough for carriages and also able to be blocked. Around the monument Downing proposed to plant "*American* trees of large growth, disposed in open groups, so as to alow of fine vistas of the Potomac river."

In his initial plan Downing did not detail what he proposed for the remainder of the White House grounds beyond deciding that nothing would remain near the mansion except the orangery. To the north he proposed simplifying the two gates and moving the drive so it would no longer pass under the portico. He envisioned extensive lawns and groupings of trees. It was just as well that he went no further, for what he did present would have required a great deal of time, money, and energy. Fillmore, based on his experiences landscaping his own home, seems to have understood very well the immensity of what Downing was projecting. The president took more than five weeks to think through the matter and concluded that he could sanction only the suggestions for the area south of the stone wall and on the Mall itself only to 7th street to the east.

Although the initial work began auspiciously enough soon after Fillmore provided the authorization, difficulties presented themselves at once to all concerned. These were centered on the chain of command. As Downing had made clear when he took the job, he would not be a full-time Washington Rural Architect; he had, after all, his own business to attend to, especially with a federal salary of only $1,500 per year. This allowed misunderstandings to develop.

For day-to-day supervision Downing relied on a foreman, William D. Brackinridge, with whom he seems to have had a good working relationship, Downing retaining full control even though he limited his on-site inspections to six-week intervals. Considering how slowly work could advance with pick, shovel, wheelbarrow, and cart, even though the number of laborers might be large, progress would be slow. It was in fact slower than anticipated.

The first task to be undertaken at the White House was south of the stone wall. Work there continued vigorously throughout 1851 in preparation for a spring planting extravaganza. Work was also pressed forward in 1852 to make way for the new statute of Andrew Jackson on horseback in Lafayette Square, the name given to the President's Park north of the mansion in honor of the French hero's visit in 1824 and 1825. It would ultimately be unveiled in January 1853 by President Fillmore. Trees planted by Charles Bulfinch during the Monroe administration were thinned to permit construction of walks to the center of the square, where the statue would be located. In the next administration, that of

Franklin Pierce, an iron fence would be built around the square, and gas lamps were added as well.

President and Mrs. Fillmore used that winter to think through renovation of the President's Garden, which they anticipated would begin in spring. The first change involved John Ousley, who in January was advised that his services would no longer be required. After twenty-five years' service in the gardens he had made his own, Ousley must have been crushed. It was not that his work was no longer considered satisfactory; Fillmore wanted someone who projected a more energetic and youthful image. He chose as a replacement an aggressive young Scot newly arrived in America, John Watt. Watt initially did routine work, waiting for the busy Downing to provide plans for Watt's domain. As it turned out, Watt would have to wait until Franklin Pierce became president to show what he could do. Jemmy Maher, although an old man too, was allowed to stay.

Meanwhile Downing was supervising the selection of plants gathered together for use in Washington by the Parsons & Co. nurseries of Flushing, New York. Thousands of trees would be needed for transplanting onto the newly graded grounds.

By the end of March 1852, thirty-three men began grading the Mall. It began to look as though Downing's plan might succeed in spite of its grandiose nature. Fate intervened. Downing and his working plans were lost when the steamer *Henry Clay* burned on the Hudson River on July 28, 1852. With the mastermind gone and so many details missing on paper (or never formulated), the project foundered. Fillmore himself knew he could not follow through. That summer the Whig Party refused to renominate him for the highest office in the land.

Franklin Pierce
1853-57

John Watt, employed as the White House gardener by Millard Fillmore, could now under Franklin Pierce show his talents while Jemmy Maher resumed direction of tree planting on both the Mall and on Washington streets. As usual, Maher used stock he had raised in his own nursery, reducing his going price of $4.00 for each sapling to $2.50. Watt had the more challenging job. More so even than northern gardens, southern gardens require constant vigilance and work if they are to remain in top-notch condition. In anticipation of Andrew Jackson Downing's landscaping revisions, the area encompassing the president's gardens had been allowed to slide. Perennial plants needed replacing. Pruning (undoubtedly forgone for too long) became of prime importance. Trellises, the arbor, and anything else made of wood needed new paint (green and white were the colors used); some needed replacing. A new white picket fence was constructed around the flower garden. Paths needed constant replenishment of gravel. Keeping lawn areas in good repair was also a continuous job. This John Watt and his assistants did well with the help of sheep outside Jefferson's wall.

Only a privileged few were allowed access to the south grounds. Mrs. Pierce usually kept to her rooms, and there is no record that the president himself enjoyed Watt's accomplishments outdoors on more than a casual basis. His interest lay in greenhouses. The White House orangery by now was no longer in style; it needed updating. Although it is unclear who first proposed a White House greenhouse, it was probably the plant-loving Fillmores or Andrew Jackson Downing, or perhaps the decision was arrived at jointly. In any event, Congress appropriated $12,000 for work on the south grounds the day before Pierce was inaugurated in 1853. This was a large sum for the era. Comparable outlays were made only when major construction work was involved. Furthermore, after Charles Ogle's blast at the Martin Van Buren administration, Congress wanted to know why so much money was being sought. But as we shall see, the legislature by now was not unfriendly to greenhouses, and much of the aforementioned money was devoted to such a structure for the White House.

Greenhouses have had a long and honorable history, the earliest being built in the first century A.D. for the Roman emperor Nero, who wanted cucumbers out of season. Small panes were fashioned from translucent sheets of mica to satisfy Nero's whim. Because of the technical difficultites involved, the first truly practical greenhouse was not constructed until 1599. The country was Holland, and the designer was the French botanist Jules Charles. The plants were medicinal in character and tropical in origin. But the real impetus for greenhouses was gastronomic. Europeans were introduced to the wonders of oranges in the Middle Ages, and in northern Europe orangeries were needed to grow them. Tall expanses of glass facing south admitted as much light as possible, with stoves providing extra heat. During warmer weather the potted plants were carried outside. Confined of course only to royalty and wealthy persons who could afford them, European orangeries were in some cases huge. One in Versailles, for example, was more than 500 feet long, 42 feet wide, and 45 feet high. Heating them was a monumental task that required constant attention.

The first American greenhouse was built by a Boston merchant, André Faneuil, before 1737. By the mid-1800s greenhouses had become almost de rigueur for affluent horticulturists, while commerical glasshouses, as they were also known, were bringing flowers into many other homes. With better glass available, roofs and all four sides could consist of panes, thereby providing more light. Together with more sophisticated heating and ventilating systems to keep temperatures stable, these structures became more versatile.

The federal government had built its first greenhouse in 1842 behind the Patent Office for plants brought back from Commodore Charles Wilkes's expedition to the Pacific. By 1850 Congress had authorized a Botanic Garden, located at the foot of Capitol Hill. The old greenhouses from the Patent Office were then moved there to serve as wings for a proposed new and larger building. This was put up by 1857 for the substantial number of plants brought by Matthew C. Perry in 1855 from his expedition to Japan.

In preparation for the construction of a modern greenhouse at the White House, John Watt under President Pierce dismantled the old orangery except for the brick walls. The orangery was in effect retained as a central brick-floored building enhanced now with iron tables and chairs surrounded by potted ferns and fruit trees for the exclusive pleasure of the president. In effect it was a mini-conservatory, a lovely retreat especially in winter. On either side were the true working greenhouses with glass roofs, sections of which could be opened by ropes and pulleys to provide better air circulation. For better heat and light the south roof sloped low, while the north wall of brick, built in Jefferson's day, projected only slightly above ground level. This helped retain heat if only by blocking the north wind. Floors in the greenhouses proper were dirt covered by moist sand. Pots stood on shelves and tables everywhere light permitted. Heat was provided by a large coal-burning furnace beneath the orangery. Water was piped in from buried cisterns.

Needless to say, Watt bought and moved in plants expeditiously as sections of the new structure were completed. Camellias were prominent, but as this area was frequented only by the president and his intimates little is known about it—particularly because it survived only four years.

The new greenhouse complex had been doomed before it was even built. The problem was the location of the Treasury Building. Treasury and State had been located to the east of the mansion with War and Navy to the west. George Washington himself had selected the sites, wanting them close to the White House rather than to the Capitol because, as President Washington pointed out, Congress was in session only part-time while the executive branch would function full-time.

The original buildings were sufficiently large for the government of the day and were nicely designed as well, but employees there found them increasingly inadequate. In 1833, adding injury to insult, the Treasury Building was destroyed by fire for the second time. (The first conflagration had been due to the British.) Actually, the second fire was providential. Toward the end of Andrew Jackson's second term, the Committee on Public Buildings met with the commissioner and representatives of the president to determine what to do. The consensus was to construct new buildings to replace all the original executive buildings that, like the Treasury, had gotten too small to perform required duties effectively. The question was where to locate the Treasury. Neither plan presented to the president met with his approval, for both crowded the White House grounds. The spot Jackson chose to the south of the old Treasury Building had one inestimable advantage. Pennsylvania Avenue would now have its architectural terminus, although not the one L'Enfant had had in mind—the White House itself. Old Hickory had thereby solved a problem that had baffled even the professionals.

Construction was begun in 1852. The so-called Jefferson mounds were built in 1855 of dirt excavated from the cellars of the new building. By the end of President Franklin Pierce's term in 1857, preparation for the Treasury extension to the north was far enough along to require removing the greenhouses. As outdoor privacy for the president was becoming more difficult to realize, what with the south grounds increasingly encroached upon, the Commissioner of Public Buildings, Dr. John Blake, decided that a new greenhouse should be built immediately, this time attached to the mansion itself. The structure would be placed over the west wing of the house. The new site would provide easy and private access to gardenlike surroundings for succeeding presidents, their families, and guests. Pierce provided encouragement and approved the plan, but as construction did not begin until James Buchanan assumed office in 1857, he did not personally benefit from it.

The greenhouse cost $16,000, even though it was made of wood, not iron as was first proposed. Entrance was through a glassed-in passage from the White House itself to a single very tall room with steep roof lines. Potted plants covered the tables with foliage and flowers. More plants hung from the ceiling in baskets while vines climbed on the wooden frame.

The ceiling had colored glass panes mixed in with the clear ones, providing unexpected elegance. Water was obtained from hydrants at each end of the room with a third in an adjacent potting shed that James Buchanan would order added to the master plan. Humidity was increased through evaporation from shallow containers of water. The same up-to-date type of heating system installed in the house in 1853 was used in the greenhouse. It was in essence a hot-water furnace with heated air rising and circulating through the big room. Cooling was provided by hinged window panes.

In early November 1857, after Buchanan had moved into the White House, John Watt was able to move his plants from the old location to the new. He must have held his breath during the months the structure was under construction, for it ended up costing $4,000 more than the appropriation had provided. (The original cost had been underestimated.) What his new domain looked like inside was unknown to everyone except the favored few who were permitted to see it. The president would have his garden in private even if it was now indoors.

On the south grounds during Franklin Pierce's tenure Watt got his president's approval for extensive renovation and repair. Plants bloomed profusely, and fresh paint adorned garden structures. Short of a master plan to revise the entire area, Watt did what all good gardeners do: He nurtured what he had.

Interim

1857-77

For gardens or landscaped grounds to remain at their peak requires constant vigilance and effort. From time to time infusions of money are required too. On public property in particular the status of horticulture reflects the public's priorities. The massive projects that were pursued prior to the Civil War would not have been undertaken afterward. Gardening was no longer in style. The agricultural background of almost all Americans, which for some spilled over into landscaping and flower gardens, was slowly giving way to an industrial society. The country came to have other matters on its mind, not the least of which was the issue of slavery, the very basis of agriculture and much of the lifestyle for large segments of the south. After the Civil War the nation itself would never be the same.

From a horticultural point of view President James Buchanan's term (1857–61) was dominated by the new greenhouse, with

Wood engraving of interior of the conservatory above the west wing of the White House, 1858. (Library of Congress)

which he was pleased. Based on observations abroad and at home he had become aware of the virtues of such a structure, not the least of which was the privacy it afforded. Buchanan extended the concept of presidential privacy in the outdoor garden areas too.

During Abraham Lincoln's term in office (1861–65) the Civil War consumed the nation's thoughts and activities. Mrs. Lincoln in particular found solace in the greenhouse and made a great friend of John Watt, the gardener, who was careful to keep her supplied with flowers for the great house. Expenditures except for maintenance were clearly out of the question during these troubled times.

Thus Andrew Johnson (1965–69), who assumed office upon Lincoln's assassination, was faced not only with the reconstruction of a country but also the reconstruction of a presidential

Photograph of interior of the conservatory. (Library of Congress)

house too long neglected. Under the direction of Johnson's able daughter Martha (his wife was in poor health), the interior of the mansion was thoroughly cleaned, painted, repaired, and refurbished where needed. The east wing Jefferson had built, battered by time, was torn down. With it gone the White House looked very bare, especially because East Executive Avenue was built to separate it from the Treasury Building (finally completed in 1869). The latter's west portico now overpowered the President's House, which was, after all, supposed to be the center of attention. To rectify this a new formal entrance to the mansion's yard was built.

An unexpected and surely unwelcome expense was the reconstruction of the greenhouse, which burned in January 1867. With winter temperatures prevailing, plants not destroyed by the fire were subject to freezing. Few probably survived the ordeal.

One of the earliest photographs of the north front, 1861. Note statue of Jefferson. (Library of Congress)

Although the new greenhouse was once again made of wood to cut costs, the roof of the west wing upon which it stood was at least reinforced for better support. If Andrew Johnson was inclined to do something further in the horticultural line, the tattered condition of the country and his own single term prevented it. Meanwhile his daughter, perfectionist that she was, appears to have taken an active interest in restocking the glasshouse. Large numbers of plants were purchased starting in the spring of 1868. Ferns of many kinds were foils for flowering and fruit-bearing specimens.

Ulysses S. Grant (1869–77), who had been a war hero, was known for a tenure marked by numerous scandals. Grant felt no constraints in setting a new tone of good feeling accompanied by

a good life dubbed the Gilded Age, which ended after the Panic of 1873 midway through his two terms in office.

On the grounds, to complete the plan begun under Andrew Johnson, West Executive Avenue was built in 1871. By 1874 the new State, War, and Navy Building was also in place, directly across West Executive Avenue from where the Executive Office Building would be constructed in 1902. With both streets joined in a semicircle to the far south, the area was now enclosed by an iron fence to match the one around the north grounds. In 1873 another drive was built, this one on the south lawn. It was in the shape of a guitar.

In 1874 Jefferson's statue, which had been placed before the north portico of the White House in 1847 by then President James K. Polk, was returned to the Capitol whence it had come.

Isometrical view of grounds. Undated, but guitar-shaped drive on south grounds built under Grant in 1873. (Library of Congress)

(Jefferson's gates had been removed during James Buchanan's term.) To replace the statue a large parterre was designed centered on a pond with a water jet. The pond survived, but the gardens proved short-lived.

Grant, who apparently did not fear for his own safety or that of his family, spent time in the President's Park for purposes of pleasure. To compensate for the new fence to the south, the upper part of Jefferson's stone wall around the inner grounds was removed so that the public, banned from the area at Mrs. Grant's request, could still see the First Family. The wall was demolished later in Grant's term.

At the far south end the public could get a close-up view of the newly installed seventy-five-foot pool with a fountain. As for the greenhouse, Grant did not neglect it, perhaps in response to his wife's love of flowers. He enlarged it over the ell of the west wing, the first of several major expansions of the facilities before they were torn down in the early 1900s.

Rutherford B. Hayes

1877 - 81

While President Grant had made some alterations in the White House landscaping, it was left for Rutherford B. Hayes to make two major decisions. One involved the area that would become known as the Ellipse; the other concerned the greenhouses, soon to be transformed into a true conservatory.

The environs of the great house had been altered dramatically since George Washington's day. No longer did the grounds front on rutted country roads sparsely sprinkled with buildings. Grading had provided a finished look, and more trees were fulfilling their potential. But the grounds were increasingly circumscribed because of building and road construction around the mansion itself. As a result, modifications to the landscaping were necessary. Preserving some semblance of privacy for the president and his family required determination and skill.

For such a transformation, two ingredients were necessary: a president who had a real interest in and knowledge of landscaping and horticulture, and a public employee of similar mind in a position to make significant changes possible. After a lapse of more than twenty-five years and the intervention of a civil war, the prerequisites again came together. Hayes was the president; Andrew Jackson Downing, although long dead, was the other. The appointment by Mrs. Hayes of an aggressive and able man, Henry Pfister, to oversee horticultural projects assured success, especially because Mrs. Hayes herself was very competent in her own right.

The construction of West Executive Avenue to match East Executive Avenue had defined the available space left around the President's House. Hayes's main interest was what to do with the large expanse beyond the semicircle south of the mansion. This area, home to feeding pens for a wartime slaughterhouse, was most unattractive, hardly fitting as a foreground to the White House from the new Washington Monument. Andrew Jackson Downing once again came to the rescue. A major part of his plan, drawn in 1851, was still appropriate, despite changes in streets and buildings made in the intervening years. This southern area he had designated as the Parade. Under Hayes the circle became a seventeen-acre level oval surrounded by a fifty-foot-wide gravel road bordered by rows of elms and shielded from the outside by masses of various types of trees. With the change of shape a change of name seemed appropriate, and the site became known as the Ellipse. It was made from fill left over from regrading associated with paving Pennsylvania Avenue, from the basement of the newly constructed State, War, and Navy Building, and from commercial companies. It was finished in 1880. The Ellipse quickly became the most popular place to see and be seen.

Andrew Jackson Downing may not have hit upon a permanent name, but he certainly correctly foresaw the appropriate use for this land connecting the White House and the Mall, even though it further reduced presidential privacy.

This major decision by Hayes was supplemented by less dramatic changes to grounds that had become dated. Renovation was in order, for few gardens and plantings remain at the peak of their potential for decades. Earlier parterres planted to the south and those planted to the north by Grant were removed and planted with grass. To provide some floral material that would always be in good condition, Hayes began the practice of putting tropical plants from the greenhouse around the pool in the center of the lawn area encompassed by the semicircular north drive. Horse chestnut trees (buckeyes) brought by the Hayeses from Ohio remained part of the landscape for many decades.

A minor project to the south was the construction of a croquet lawn. To make room for it, a fountain that Andrew Johnson had built next to the south portico was dismantled and installed in Grant's pool at the south edge of the lawn. The fountain from that pool was used for the pool to the north of the mansion, which had also been built in the Grant administration.

A more lasting change outdoors was inaugurated by the Hayeses. Rolling Easter eggs on Easter Monday had long been an accepted activity on the Capitol grounds until Congress banned it in 1878. This annual event was now scheduled for the south lawn of the White House. In the Hayes era the children numbered only a few hundred. By 1893 there were an estimated 20,000. Even with the protection of fences around flower beds and vulnerable trees and shrubs, the south grounds suffered considerable damage every year—especially the lawns, which routinely needed resodding or reseeding.

Because of fears for presidential security, the Hayeses took a great interest in the greenhouse. The family walked there after breakfast, Mrs. Hayes remaining to help arrange flowers for the mansion and select bouquets for friends and for patients in Washington's hospitals.

It was during the Hayes administration that the White House greenhouse became a conservatory in the modern sense. Hayes's ability to be innovative and think on a grand scale extended to the indoors. In this he was ably assisted by his wife and Henry Pfister. Lucy Hayes in fact chose enlargement of the conservatory over redecoration and repairs to the interior of the house, necessary as these were. Her love of flowers was responsible for the delegation of one of every four dollars appropriated for maintenance of the White House to the upkeep of the glasshouses.

There were two notable extensions to the greenhouse complex. The first was built in 1878 as a separate glasshouse for roses on ground level below the main structure on the site of the Rose Garden developed later by President John Kennedy. As it had no floor, the bushes could be planted directly in the ground, although some were planted in tubs. Paved walks permitted access to the building. Shade from summer sunlight streaming through the roof was provided by canvas awnings unrolled to meet the need, while air circulation was increased by opening a pair of large glass doors. The roses in tubs were moved outdoors during the warmest months, reminiscent of the practice used in the old orangery. Mrs. Hayes would retain her love for roses. The day of her fatal stroke she was going through a catalogue trying to decide if there were any varieties she did *not* want to order.

The second extension involved the narrow glassed passageway that had been built to provide access to the main greenhouse from the west end of the mansion. President Grant was in office by the time this area was reconstructed after the fire in the Johnson years. Billiard rooms being popular, Grant used this hallway for one. Although Hayes wanted a billiard room too, he would not waste such valuable space so ideal for enlarging the greenhouse. The structure was thus torn down, and a billiard room was built on the basement level. The new greenhouse, now named the conservatory promenade, was constructed with an iron frame, the only sensible thing to do despite the added expense.

Once again there would be an unbroken view to the north and south from walls of glass. Even better, both of the west windows of the state dining room, which had been plastered over to make the billiard room, were now uncovered and made into French doors, thereby providing direct access to the horticultural display. The area became a delightful and important adjunct to the dining room to replace after-dinner drinking in accordance with Temperance Union agitation. When the meal was finished, guests were led by the Hayeses on a tour down one long aisle and back on the second of the horseshoe-shaped walk paved with encaustic tiles. With the center bounteously filled with palms and ferns, which screened one aisle from the other, the walk must have seemed more secluded than it really was. The illusion was enhanced by the banks of flowers on the stepped tables along the north and south walls, which had elegant views of the grounds as their backdrop.

This same attention to aesthetics was extended to the greenhouse proper, which became the main conservatory. (There were in fact a dozen buildings in all.) Certainly a motivating factor here in the layout was the sheer size and shapes of women's dresses. Narrow aisles were not conducive to free movement by the ladies; the aisles were therefore widened. With more space available it was possible to introduce iron benches at appropriate spots, ornamental plant stands, and other methods of displaying plants more artistically. The outdoors were truly brought inside, and with an enclosed building the space could be used agreeably in all seasons by the president, his family, and, when he chose, his guests.

The conservatory was responsible for the inspiration of another type of design, the Haviland & Co. china set purchased for the White House by the Hayes administration. For the artwork Mrs. Hayes chose Theodore R. Davis for his wide knowledge of American plants and animals. The design for the china began innocuously enough with ferns from the glasshouse, but Davis expanded it to include a depiction of a wide variety of plants and animals. The novelty of this approach gained widespread attention if not admiration. The conservatory itself seems to have been beyond reproach. Unfortunately, it remained in existence only two more decades.

Interim

1 8 8 1 - 1 9 0 1

Not until Grover Cleveland came to office in 1885 did Henry Pfister again have an accomplice in maintaining his glasshouses. Cleveland enjoyed flowers, an interest he had developed while governor of New York. The mansion in Albany had a small conservatory. Although this interest at the White House was confined to his using the greenhouses for a change of pace, the president encouraged Pfister to make the conservatory even better than it already was. (In Cleveland's second term, following that of Benjamin Harrison, his new wife made extensive use of the conservatory.)

Benjamin Harrison (1889–93) was not concerned with horticulture. However, his wife, Caroline, was—to the extent that plants formed the subject matter for her watercolors and paintings on china. She was particularly partial to orchids and popularized this flower. She thus made continuous use of the conservatory

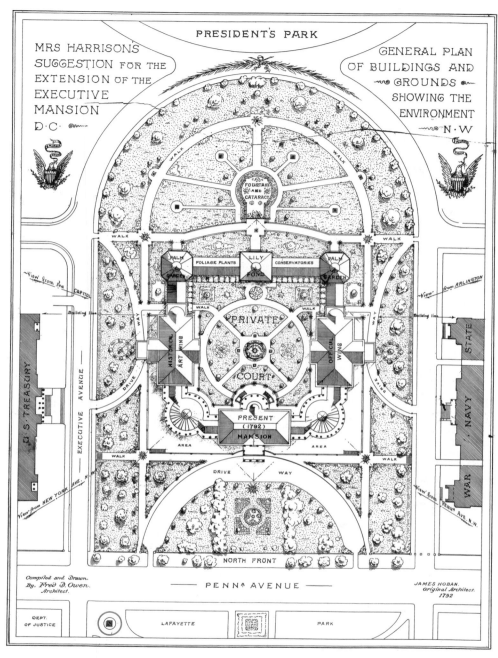

Caroline Harrison's proposed expansion of mansion complex, 1891. (National Archives)

North front, 1891.
(Library of
Congress)

and gardens. (Mrs. Harrison was also responsible for a new china set of dinnerware. Her design was based on sweet corn and goldenrod—unlikely subject material, perhaps, but the finished pieces were approved by those who saw them.)

Caroline Harrison's greater talent lay in thinking big. Her husband had assumed office in 1889, one hundred years after George Washington had taken the first presidential oath. The nation of course celebrated this centennial. Although the interest of most people was confined to the history of the past, Mrs. Harrison looked toward the future.

George Washington had foreseen that the White House design produced in his day by James Hoban would at some point become inadequate. L'Enfant, the first architect called upon to prepare a plan, had not been wrong in proposing a "palace." In the decades preceding President Harrison's tenure there had been agitation for a larger building, especially one more in proportion to the site. Plans were contemplated, even drawn, some based on the existing structure, others for a brand-new one in a different location. Mrs. Harrison's vision went one step further, for it enlarged not only Hoban's house but also the conservatory.

The resulting proposal designed by a Washington engineer, Frederick D. Owen, called for a large wing to the south of the house at both the east and west ends. The existing mansion, serving as a center for the complex to the north, was matched on the south by an elaborate pair of glassed buildings designated as palm gardens joined by a long conservatory unit that provided, at its center, an attractive exit to the south grounds. Because of the slope, the conservatory unit was at a lower level than the White

Another view of the clutter confronting Charles F. McKim, landscape architect under Theodore Roosevelt, on the north front. Note the conservatory on the right. (Library of Congress)

House itself, thereby permitting an unobstructed view from the south windows of the mansion.

Although Mrs. Harrison's design was not acted upon because of political reasons unrelated to the plan itself, it served as an impetus to commence what was becoming inevitable: an expansion of the White House complex. The country was growing up and getting more populous as well.

Theodore Roosevelt
1 9 0 1 - 9

The proposed expansion of the White House by the gifted Caroline Harrison (who had dared to intrude onto traditionally male turf) was resurrected in 1900 by Colonel Theodore Bingham, now the officer in charge of public buildings. The occasion was the one hundredth anniversary of John and Abigail Adams's move into the new mansion. Bingham thought this would be an auspicious time to push for an enlarged executive unit. To this end he got President William McKinley to back a bill that appropriated funds to work on such plans. Bingham's instrument was the Corps of Engineers, which had been responsible for the nation's public buildings since Andrew Johnson's day.

Bingham was confronted with an unlikely opponent in pursuit of his goal: Mary Foote Henderson, a Washington philanthropist. As the widow of a prominent senator, she had good connections as well as a great deal of money. Backed by the expertise of

Paul J. Pelz, co-architect of the Library of Congress, she set forth to get her conception of the White House approved. Her fortune and influence notwithstanding, Bingham won the mini-war.

The colonel then turned to Frederick D. Owen, who had drawn the plans for Mrs. Harrison, and together the two engineers updated the original proposal. A scale model was made and put on display at the White House the day of the anniversary celebration, December 12, 1900. It drew immediate criticism from the architectural community, which was struggling to be recognized professionally. To add to Bingham's problems, by March 1901 Mrs. McKinley had become ill, never to really recover, and by September the president himself was dead of an assassin's bullet.

Bingham's plan soon ran into a more formidable snag than mere illness and death and even a new president, Theodore Roosevelt, might suggest. He might even have survived the wrath of individual architects who felt that they had been neglected, if not usurped. He could not survive the consequences of making an enemy of a powerful senator, James McMillan, who also happened to be the chairman of the Centennial Committee. McMillan, no stranger to the field of urban planning, found an ally in the American Institute of Architects, which agreed that, considering monetary restrictions, the first order of business at this point in time was a master plan for the public lands in the rapidly growing city of Washington, recovering as much of L'Enfant's original ideas as possible. A distinguished group of four consultants was named to form what became known as the McMillan Commission: David H. Burnham, Frederick Law Olmsted, Jr., Charles F. McKim, and Augustus Saint-Gaudens.

Several results stemmed from the formation of this committee. A seven-week tour in Europe was taken by the first three (with Charles Moore, McMillan's political secretary, as his personal representative) to observe relevant great houses, gardens, and cities. There was a temporary slip by Burnham into the blind alley of advocating the relocation of the White House to the site of the Old Naval Observatory. A reappraisal of L'Enfant's plan followed.

Finally the commission issued a report that on January 15, 1902, was agreed to unanimously by the Senate Committee on the District of Columbia. Downing's 1851 plan for the Mall was abandoned. In truth at this point there was no possibility that the Mall could be restored to the rural character of Downing's day. By 1872, for example, under Grant the Pennsylvania Railroad station had been built, and tracks were laid across the Mall at 6th Street. With all the facilities that develop around and to serve such an enterprise, the Mall could never again revert to even semiseclusion even though the station was torn down and the tracks were removed by 1910. Instead the Mall was extended to the river itself. On the new western extension, the Lincoln Memorial was built by 1922. The old Tiber canal was destroyed by paving over it; the source of the water leading to it was diverted, effectively eliminating flooding. Implementation of other parts of the McMillan Commission plan would similarly take years.

McKim emerged as the strongest member of the McMillan Commission, but his first job was restoring and enlarging the White House, and to that end he had to devote considerable time. Once again a woman assumed leadership, this time Edith Kermit Roosevelt, the president's wife. It was she who sought the help of McKim, whose considerable reputation for expertise in such matters commended him for the formidable job of revitalizing the President's House. The cost would be enormous, and there was no consensus as to what changes to make, for James Hoban's original design was by now almost sacred. The Roosevelts, however, succeeded where others had failed, as much because of their desire to return the mansion to the Hoban spirit as to their undoubted ability to be forceful leaders. In addition, for them the need to expand touched every facet of their daily lives. The Roosevelts had six young children to accommodate. The nation for its part had continued to grow, and this increased presidential responsibilities. Increasing numbers of office holders, employees, guests, and the just plain curious demanded access to the White House—their house.

It was important to get modifications to the mansion finalized before working on the grounds, and the Roosevelts understood that. By now it was evident that an executive office building was absolutely essential to replace the White House itself as the site for purely business purposes. But removal of the conservatory from the west wing of the house was also seen by McKim as necessary. He did not like glasshouses as adjuncts to buildings. Nothing should detract from the mansion itself.

Despite the disrepair of the conservatory and its adjacent

Conservatory and greenhouses, 1901. (Library of Congress)

facilities, both Roosevelts protested at first. They had grown up together as best friends, and both had developed a deep-seated love of the natural world. While Theodore had leaned more toward zoology, Edith as a teenager had taught herself the names of plants as she collected them in rambles in the New Jersey countryside. By adulthood she was able to identify even the most obscure. She would not give up the greenhouses easily, not so much because she enjoyed wandering through them as for their wealth of plant material for cut flowers and decorating the house with foliage plants such as palms. Yet she understood that from an architectural point of view the greenhouses were not Hoban.

Henry Pfister, still the head gardener from the Hayes era, was beside himself. He could not abandon the plants he had collected and labored with for well over two decades, but ultimately he too bowed to the inevitable; he had no choice.

The conservatory and working areas had served the occupants of the White House well, as a place to escape and of course for the flowers and decorative plants it provided to adorn people, tables, and entire rooms at virtually a moment's notice. Without these facilities flowers and potted plants would have to be purchased or loaned from a commerical establishment. Ultimately a compromise was worked out. This was the famous Treaty of Oyster Bay, which pitted Colonel Theodore Bingham, still pursuing Caroline Harrison's goal of extensive greenhouses, against Charles McKim. At a meeting with Edith at the Roosevelts' Sagamore Hill, McKim got concessions he, as the architect, could live with.

Using materials that could be salvaged, a greenhouse was constructed near the Washington Monument on the propagating grounds. In order to make up for the loss of the larger conservatory, McKim had offered Edith a small but artistic glasshouse for purposes of pleasure only, but she turned it down. There was, after all, a public budget to consider, and it was fast reaching its limits. Edith Kermit Roosevelt was very conscious of budgets.

As it was, because of insufficient funds the interior of the White House was not rebuilt as it should have been considering the age of the mansion and previous renovations. (Some forty-five years later, under President Harry Truman, the job was eventually redone.) Nevertheless, McKim's plan bought some very necessary borrowed time for the old house. And under the domination of one man it now presented a unified decoration of the entire interior instead of the hodgepodge evident before. Outside, with the greenhouses gone, the new executive office building could be seen from the north front, but as it was supposed to be temporary in nature this did not give McKim any concern. It was a one-story structure connected to Jefferson's west wing, now restored.

The east wing, torn down in 1866, was rebuilt by McKim. It was entered through a graceful colonnaded porte cochere from which visitors could enter the White House. Between it and East Executive Avenue was a circular fountain, a set of stairs, and an ornamental cast-iron gate. The walk from the gate to the door was divided by a flower bed. To blend the unit into the mansion the top of this one-story structure was made into an open-air promenade with box trees softening the view from the mansion windows. Deliveries were made now via a new driveway under the North Portico instead of at the front door.

With plans for the house finished, McKim could turn to the grounds. Not much land was left to work with. Current architectural thinking made the house the center of all landscaping with nothing to hide it unless it had some unpleasing feature. The

White House did not. McKim's solution was to plant many trees and shrubs to frame the house, particularly on the private south grounds. There was no question of the necessity of removing the flower beds north of the mansion. Their sheer extravagance of plants and design made for an uncoordinated appearance. Colonel Bingham reported in November 1901 that there were 66 beds planted with 64,000 early spring bulbs and 5,000 spring flowering plants. In May these were replaced by summer flowering and foliage plants. This clutter would go.

To satisfy his immediate boss, Mrs. Roosevelt, if not through his own conviction of their merits, McKim planned two formal gardens directly south of the colonnades at the back of the house, one adjacent to the east wing and one adjacent to the west wing. The latter Edith Kermit Roosevelt claimed as her own. In view of the return to an eighteenth-century mode for the White House, it was to be an old-fashioned colonial garden, a geometric parterre with intersecting paths and outlined with boxwood. The interiors of each of the four giant petals that formed the unit were filled with flowers. This was quite a change for the site on which the rose glasshouse had stood. The *Christian Science Monitor* reported that little walks were arranged all through the beds containing old-fashioned perennials such as phlox, forget-me-nots, wall flowers, delphinium, English hardy daisies, irises, and a few roses. Mrs. Roosevelt, said the newspaper, liked fresh flowers brought to her suite every morning.

The second garden was also in the colonial theme. The other parterres were replaced with clusters of low evergreens.

Wife and husband routinely walked the gardens after breakfast. Although never the active gardener, as several First Ladies have been, Mrs. Roosevelt is known to have planted bulbs after leaving the White House, and upon the birth of a granddaughter in 1911 planted a little grove of pines at the family estate at Sagamore Hill in New York.

Presidents dating back to Jefferson had retreated to their personal homes from time to time to escape their jobs temporarily, particularly in the summer when swampy lands near the White House grounds became breeding grounds for diseases. Without air conditioning, the heat and humidity of Washington would have been reason enough to leave. Such a strategy was feasible only as long as presidential tasks did not require more or less full-time attendance in the capital and the president concerned lived not too far away. Improved roads and transportation eased the latter problem somewhat, but the former got worse with the passing of the years. Being president had become a full-time job.

In addition, the Roosevelts found the press, politicians, office seekers, and total strangers constantly at their door at Sagamore Hill as well as in Washington as presidents before them had experienced at their respective private homes. Jefferson, who treasured his solitude, responded by building out-of-the-way Poplar Forest in Bedford County, Virginia. At the other extreme the James Madisons bore up, Dolley thriving on people. While Theodore Roosevelt loved being with people too, his wife was much more reserved. Fortunately for their marriage, Theodore could also immerse himself in solitude and flourish.

Once again Edith took the initiative to resolve this problem. After a cruise through the St. John's River wilderness in Florida, in April 1905, she determined to find a weekend hideaway near Washington. An old family friend had an unused three-room house on his 500-acre estate 125 miles from Washington in Jefferson's Albemarle County. Would she be interested? Edith took the train from Washington, was driven some ten miles, then walked alone the last mile, crossing a brook before getting to the cabin's door. Without hesitation she promptly agreed to pay $195 for the dwelling plus five acres.

That June, Edith took her husband to see the place. Theodore was ecstatic despite the fact that the house was much more dilapidated than it was merely rustic. Ever the outdoorsman, he reveled in the challenge to make do, as did Edith herself.

Few were invited to Pine Knot, as Edith named the place. The naturalist John Burroughs was one. He was surprised (although he should not have been) that of the seventy-five species of birds he and the president saw on a hike through the property his host could name seventy-three at once. Burroughs was somewhat chagrined that he could not name the other two himself. The president one-upped him on the question of flying squirrels. The naturalist found a nest in his bedroom and took it down because the animals were disturbing him. The Roosevelts promptly replaced the nest and its two occupants in their own room.

Cousin Franklin Delano Roosevelt would later have his Shangri-la, renamed Camp David by Dwight Eisenhower and used as a presidential retreat ever since. Washington, D.C., not to mention the White House grounds themselves, could no longer provide sufficient refreshment.

Even at Sagamore Hill Theodore, ever exuberant, could describe life there:

We love all the seasons; the snows and bare woods of winter; the rush of growing things and the blossom-spray of spring; the yellow grain in the ripening fruits and tasseled corn, and the deep leafy shades that are heralded by "the green dance of summer" and the sharp fall winds that tear the brilliant banners with which the trees greet the dying year.[1]

Woodrow Wilson
1913 - 21

With the greenhouses no longer an integral part of the mansion, gardeners in the White House were, short of tearing up expanses of lawn, confined to expressing themselves with what little space was left outdoors. Ellen Wilson was the next member of a presidential family to enjoy growing plants. She painted them as well. As the president's wife she was given the necessary support for her ideas, honed through experience at her home in Princeton, New Jersey, where her gardens were judged prime examples of what gardens should be. Edith Kermit Roosevelt's designs were too casual for Ellen Wilson, who preferred a more formal style in keeping with the new spirit dominating landscape architecture. While many gardeners are unaware of or ignore trends, the fact remains that styles do change in both gardens and landscaping—as Congressman Charles Ogle noted sarcastically on the floor of the House so long ago. Ellen Wilson was a leader. She also

Beatrix Farrand rendering of east garden, 1913. (College of Environmental Design/University of California, Berkeley)

happened to be partial to roses. The west garden would be devoted to them. As roses have always been a favorite of women in general and the few men who spend time working in flower beds, the president's wife received general acclaim despite the destruction of gardens so recently created.

Mrs. Wilson's second concern was the fact that the president en route to the executive office building passed through the west wing of the White House, which now housed service rooms. This offended her sense of propriety: The president of a great nation should have a better view than this on his way to work. The garden area to the east was not often used. Yet it was on constant display to the many visitors who passed through the new wing. Therefore, it too demanded attention.

Albeit her endeavors were not on a grand scale, Mrs. Wilson understood that ill-considered additions even to a small garden area can lead to disunity, an offense to an artistic sense of propriety. Americans are prone, for example, to locate a tree or shrub almost anywhere in a yard without thought as to how it relates to other trees and shrubs, not to mention buildings. This is true with flowers too. Better to dig everything out and start

over, especially when a change in mood is wanted—and Mrs. Wilson wanted a change. No colonial gardens for her.

She called upon two professionals to help flesh out her own ideas of what should be done. After all this was not a private home. One of these professionals, Beatrix Farrand, was one of the first women to make a name for herself in a field heretofore dominated by men. She was asked to plan the east garden. George Burnap was given the task of implementing Mrs. Wilson's ideas for the west garden, which was beneath her dressing room windows.

Farrand had the easier job, for Mrs. Wilson appears to have had no special ideas for the east site. As Farrand conceived it, the area would be bounded on all four sides by beds. At the center would be a rectangular lily pool surrounded by four L-shaped

Photograph of Farrand garden, 1917. (Library of Congress)

parterres. With ivy borders and many evergreens to set off the lawn, no matter what the season, the view from the south windows would be not only presentable but also inviting. The plan's other major recommendation was the fact that except for the pool it would cost little to implement.

Burnap was confronted with Mrs. Wilson's more grandiose ideas for the west garden as well as the knowledge that funds were limited. Mrs. Wilson for her part appears not to have been aware beforehand of the probable costs of the various parts of her vision. She wanted no less than to create a new walk for the president in a garden setting. Burnap obliged with sketches of an allée of clipped trees (probably projected as beech) with the entwined branches arching over the walk to provide shade during the hot summer months. An English box hedge would further

Ellen Wilson's rose garden, 1913. Note statue of Pan at far end. (Library of Congress)

screen the walk from the west wing colonnade. At the west end of the walk Burnam designed an elaborate new entrance to the executive office building. To provide an extension to the south ell at the west end of the west wing (first constructed as a stable for James Monroe's horses) and a suitable backdrop for the west end of the garden area, a wooden lattice arbor was designed. This lattice arbor served another function, effectively masking the drying yard that occupied the ground where the new Oval Office would be located in 1934. A statue of Pan in the recess of the arbor became the western focal point of Mrs. Wilson's rose garden, which was built in 1913.

At the east end, a semicircle with a high hedge balanced the bay of the arbor to the west. At the base of the hedge a curved wooden bench with a round table in front provided a visual anchor to the ground. To tie the unit together Burnap used beds backed by formally pruned hedges to form the long sides.

When the bids came in, it was evident that plans for the west garden area would have to be modified. The elaborate entrance to the executive office building was abandoned, as was the tree-lined allée. Along the path, hedges were substituted for the trees, and the arbor at the west end was simplified. The semicircle planned for the east became a semi-octagon with a corresponding change in shape to the bench and table.

Unfortunately the first Mrs. Wilson died during her tenure as First Lady, but she accomplished a great deal.

White House, 1917. (Library of Congress)

180

SEVENTEEN

Franklin Delano Roosevelt
1933-45

It is hardly surprising that FDR would take an interest in the subject of plants. Born the only child of wealthy parents, he grew up on a Hudson River estate. As he was always asking questions, his mother and father had little trouble in urging upon him information he would need about farming and forestry to manage the approximately 400 acres he would one day inherit. The inspection trips of the farm the boy took with his father provided no dirt-on-the-hands experience, but early on FDR understood the importance of agriculture and something of the problems faced by farmers of the era. Although he traveled widely abroad with his parents throughout his childhood, at heart he remained a country boy keenly interested in the plants and animals he saw at Springwood in Hyde Park, New York. In short, he became an environmentalist at an early age.

Hyde Park would remain his center of interest. He went

there to oversee his tree plantings, as many as 50,000 in one year. He personally supervised the repair of other eroded soils on his farm. He enjoyed seeing the dogwood blooming, getting up early in the morning to bird watch, and listening to the songs that filled the air. He was eventually able to identify countless birds, trees, and other wild things. His mind, ever curious, soaked up information in all fields.

When FDR became president the country was in turmoil, and many things competed for his attention. An immediate concern was the deplorably crowded situation he found in the executive offices. FDR insisted on more working space, so in 1934 he called upon Eric Gugler, an architect, to redesign the old executive office building that Herbert Hoover had remodeled and enlarged in 1929 but that had burned later that year with considerable damage. It was reconstructed at that time to its previous size and shape even though in its six-and-a-half months of actual use the enlarged building still did not provide adequate space.

Gugler also made some sketches for redesigning the Rose Garden to conform to the measurements of the new executive office building. As a basis he expanded the existing garden to the south to line up with the south line of the addition. However, the president was not impressed with these plans.

About that time FDR met Frederick Law Olmsted, Jr., by then dean of American landscape architects, who had followed in his father's illustrious footsteps. The son had been a member of the McMillan Commission during Theodore Roosevelt's administration. Especially in view of the larger executive office building and a new east wing the president had in mind, FDR wanted to know what should be done to the White House grounds.

While the architect looked into the historical reasons for the

North front, 1934. (Library of Congress)

older plant material put in under earlier chief executives, he had more than sentiment in mind when he developed his own plan. Although he was well aware of the stir John D. Rockefeller, Jr., was creating with the reconstruction of Williamsburg, he thought something different was needed at the White House. Unlike Charles F. McKim in Theodore Roosevelt's administration, Olmsted, like FDR himself, was more concerned with presidential privacy and security than historical accuracy.

He agreed with McKim's thesis that the White House should be the center of attention with nothing to detract from its form. Yet there had been too many attempts on presidential lives, and with the conservatory gone, so was the one area heads of state, their wives, and children could go to enjoy even semi-natural surroundings without being under the prying eyes of the public.

However, Olmsted felt that he must balance this concern with the fact that the White House was not a private home, nor were its grounds private. The ambitious plan he created came to be known as the Olmsted plan and forms the basis of White House landscaping to this day.

The architect's solution was to retain the trees and shrubs that were well placed to achieve his goal of a broad expanse of lawn bordered by very thick plantings. Everything else would be removed. Over the years trees and shrubs had been planted and flower beds created that reflected the whims of a current president or gardener but were without regard to an overall plan.

In particular Olmsted did not like how the driveway on the south grounds constructed under Ulysses S. Grant cut into the lawn, so he designed an oval road centered on the South Portico of the mansion that extended southward to gates providing entrance to both East and West Executive avenues. To connect the two entrance gates he proposed a road at a lower grade level so that the sweep of lawn would be unbroken. The architect recommended other various drives to preserve the view of the White House and facilitate traffic flow. On some of these there was no consensus, and indeed it is unlikely that anyone's proposals to control automobiles in the vicinity of the mansion would satisfy everyone.

Less controversial than some of the roads was the replacement of the iron fence around the grounds. Part of it dated to Monroe's time, another to Grant's tenure. However, the old gates between their stone posts were preserved, a nice gesture to tradition. The two flower beds against the east and west wings were retained and enlarged. FDR enjoyed looking out his windows to see the current blooms.

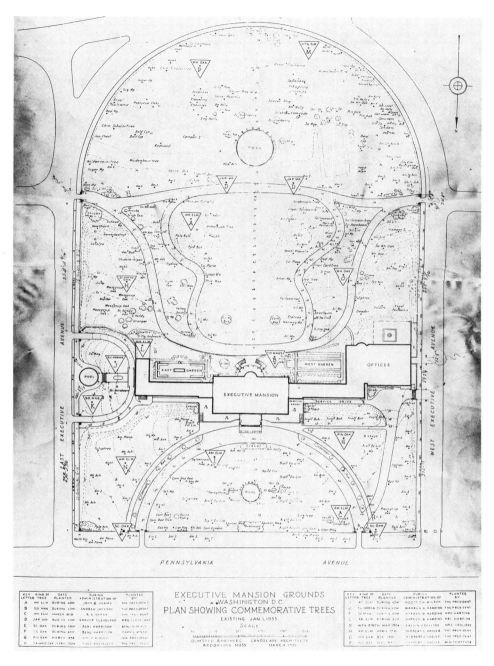

One of several plans drawn by Frederick Law Olmsted, Jr., for FDR (overall view).
(Library of Congress)

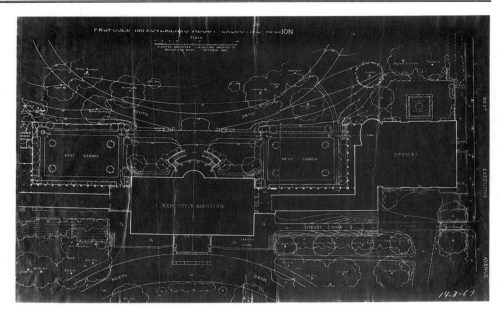

Details of Olmsted plan for area around the mansion. (National Archives)

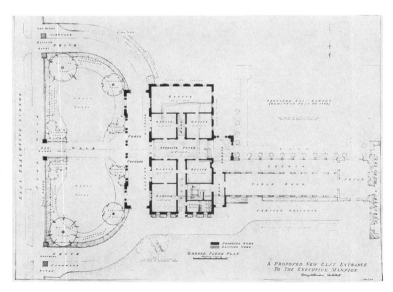

Details of Olmsted plan for new east entrance. (National Archives)

Work on Olmsted's plan was begun as soon as it was accepted. It took years to accomplish many of those parts that were not ultimately dropped.

A pleasant custom that had begun on the site of Lafayette Square was now transferred to the south grounds: lighting of the national Christmas tree. During wartime, with a blackout in effect, FDR was still adamant that this symbol be lit. He refused to consider advice to cancel the event, but he did accept this change of location so that crowds could be better controlled. For the safety of the presidential party, only those with invitations were permitted on the south lawn. Everyone else was kept outside the fence.

FDR's lifelong priorities were reflected to the end. He was buried, as he himself had specified, in the rose garden at his home at Hyde Park.

South grounds, 1946. (Library of Congress)

After FDR

Two presidents have been elected since FDR's time who are noteworthy for their horticultural undertakings. John F. Kennedy (1961–63) along with his wife, Jacqueline, wanted changes to the gardens south of the mansion. Lyndon Baines Johnson (1963–69) and his wife, Lady Bird, created a children's garden next to the tennis court and gave it as a Christmas gift to the White House. The motives of the two couples were quite different.

JFK was concerned because there was no suitable setting for the more intimate ceremonies he wished to conduct outdoors. After the reconstruction of the great house during the Truman era, the area behind the mansion had frankly deteriorated. Mrs. Paul Mellon, whom JFK asked to redesign both gardens, described what she saw as "several rows of privet hedge, Tom Thumb roses, poverty-stricken grass, and a few benches."[1] Even if the president did not expect to hold ceremonies and greet

Rachel Lambert Mellon's Rose Garden, created for JFK, 1961. (National Park Service)

guests outside as he had seen done on a recent state tour to Europe, he wanted something nicer to look out onto from the Oval Office. According to Mrs. Mellon, Jack Kennedy took endless interest in building this garden.

Mrs. Mellon, a personal friend of the Kennedys, was not a professional landscape architect, but the president and his wife obviously thought highly of her abilities nonetheless. While Mrs. Mellon was at first dubious about her qualifications for the undertaking and called upon Perry Wheeler, a friend and landscape architect practicing in Washington, for support, the resulting design was of her own creation. Amateur landscapers, both men and women, had successfully met the challenge of such an important assignment before and without exception had done very well at the task.

Mrs. Mellon found herself confronted with much White House history in the process of the garden's construction. Surprises occurred when the old soil was replaced with new. As the area was dug to a depth of four inches, many relics of bygone years, such as pieces of pots from the old greenhouses and Civil War horseshoes, were recovered. The biggest surprise of all was a cable of undetermined significance in one corner of the plot. It was cut—and the diggers were immediately surrounded by security guards. Unbeknownst to the crew or Mrs. Mellon, this cable was part of the hotline that set off the nation's military alert. (In the haste of installing it during World War II its location had not been accurately recorded.)

The west garden as Mrs. Mellon designed it was some 100 feet long and 50 feet wide. The lawn in the middle was flanked on the north and south by planting beds. Each bed, surrounded by a small hedge, had five Katherine crab apples spaced along its length. A Magnolia soulangeana was sited at each corner. In searching for suitable specimens Mrs. Mellon discovered four perfectly shaped trees near the Tidal Basin on public property. Another hedge enclosed the east and west ends of the garden with a flagstone terrace in the center of each to provide formal entrances. The trees were provided with an underplanting of a variety of flowers. The entire unit (125 feet by 60 feet) was outlined by yet another hedge.

The east garden, of comparable size, featured a pool at one end and a pergola at the other. It too was built around a central lawn area. Instead of crabs for the centers of each bed Mrs. Mellon used topiary American holly trees bordered once again by a hedge, as was the entire unit.

In spring, bulbs provided color: jonquil, daffodil, tulip, grape hyacinth, fritillaria, squill, and chinodoxa. Roses chosen for the west garden included grandiflora rose "Queen Elizabeth," hybrid tea roses "Pascale," and "King's Ransom" and shrub rose "Nevada." A variety of summer blooming annuals and perennials completed the picture in both gardens. A few herbs in the east unit were included for use by the White House chef.

The west garden has retained its identity as the Rose Garden through succeeding administrations. The east garden became known as the First Lady's Garden and was officially declared The Jacqueline Kennedy Garden by Lady Bird Johnson in 1963 in tribute to her predecessor's interest in promoting gardening at the White House.

The Johnsons, on the other hand, much as they might have appreciated what had been done during the Kennedy era, were primarily concerned with future generations when they designed their garden at the mansion. LBJ and his wife believed that children should learn to appreciate their botanical heritage. This educational theme would touch the lives of all Americans, and it dominated much of what this couple did both in the White House and afterward.

During her husband's years in office, Lady Bird initiated important projects of her own. Her childhood had been spent in the country "rather alone," as she tells it. Walking the woods observing wildflowers was a favorite pastime. In Washington she had gardened in her own yard, but when she became First Lady a new world of opportunity opened up. She felt that she owed a debt to the natural world, which had meant so much to her over the years. Now she was in a position to repay the debt.

Her activities were varied. For the mansion itself she chose a new china dinner service. The White House had been without an adequate set for years. As Lucy Hayes and Caroline Harrison had done before her, Mrs. Johnson adopted a design based on the natural world: an American eagle and wildflowers.

With Secretary of the Interior Stewart Udall, she set up the Committee for a More Beautiful Capital, which relied on private donations to upgrade the sightliness of Washington. Considerable landscaping was done. Many thousands of trees and shrubs were planted, as were almost two million bulbs, not to mention annual flowers. Parks, schools, and playgrounds benefited, as did entire neighborhoods. Even better, the beautification efforts by the committee soon caught the attention of people throughout the country.

Mrs. Johnson spent a great deal of time and energy promoting highway attractiveness. In 1965 Congress passed the necessary legislation with some personal hard lobbying by Mrs. Johnson. The First Lady was gratified the act mandated that twenty-five cents of every dollar spent for landscaping be used for native plants. The total number of acres bordering our highways and byways is staggering, and Mrs. Johnson saw clearly the possibilities of influencing a large part of America.

At age seventy she put her own personal stamp on these lands and many others by establishing in 1982 the National Wildflower Research Center in Austin, Texas. A gift from her of $125,000 was matched by Laurence Rockefeller, a committee member. Additional donations soon brought the center into being. It now serves as a clearinghouse for information on wildflowers in all fifty states and a catalyst for their propagation and preservation.

To round out her career as a conservationist Mrs. Johnson also wrote articles and, with a coauthor, a book, *Wildflowers Across*

America. Her name was given to a grove of trees in Redwood National Park, which, because of her husband's direct interest, was established in 1968.

LBJ also strongly backed almost 300 other conservation and beautification acts, fifty of which were major in scope. With his direct support, more than 1 million acres were added to the National Parks system. Also, $15 million was authorized to provide for the protection of fish and wildlife threatened with extinction. Legislation concerning air and water pollution was passed.

A children's garden on the White House grounds made a statement that needed to be made, but the programs cited previously provided some much-needed help in rescuing a nation increasingly beleaguered by "progress." It was important to make the grounds around the President's House attractive. In addition, LBJ saw the greater importance in making America itself comely once again.

In a speech soon after his election in 1964, LBJ reminded his listeners that while it was necessary to keep America strong and free, it was also necessary to keep America beautiful. He listed some of the areas in which we as Americans had failed: We had polluted our air and water; our national parks were overcrowded; our forests and other natural spots were fast being destroyed. We must, he said, put a stop to making America ugly, for once they are lost, unspoiled landscapes can never be restored to their pristine beauty. And without pristine beauty a man's spirit will wither and his sustenance will be wasted.

Except from James Madison, never had Americans heard such a clear statement from a president about the degradation of their environment. Like James Madison, LBJ did something about it.

Future presidents will face a dilemma if they are at all concerned about landscaping and gardening. The White House grounds are now surrounded by roads, buildings, and large monuments. They are also so circumscribed by historical precedent that it is difficult to believe any significant changes will be made to them, at least in the immediate future. The east and west gardens to the south of the mansion may be redesigned, flower species may be changed, but the beds themselves are likely to remain in the same locations. As individual trees and shrubs die they will undoubtedly be replaced. Any large-scale removal of healthy specimens, especially those designated as commemorative trees, would be unthinkable.

Olmsted's plan, created almost six decades ago, will probably remain the framework for the White House grounds, for it has two important virtues. First, its formality harks back to our beginnings as a nation. Americans have become more interested in and appreciative of this heritage and the remarkable group of Founding Fathers who gave it to the nation. Second, in a world in which violent acts are now commonplace and security must be the overriding concern for all presidents, the Olmsted plan provides a rational solution to the problem of providing the greatest degree of safety for the First Family together with maximum public visibility of our President's House.

Fortunately, after two centuries of existence the White House remains the familiar and symbolic house it was to be. George Washington would still recognize the outlines of the executive home he laid out so many years ago and so he likely would feel comfortable with and approve of the grounds today.

South lawn, 1982.
(National Park
Service)

Aerial view of grounds, 1982. (National Park Service)

NOTES

1. GEORGE WASHINGTON

1. John Frederick Schroeder, comp., *Maxims of George Washington* (Mt. Vernon, Va.: Mt. Vernon Ladies' Association, 1989), 127.

2. Ann Leighton, *American Gardens in the 18th Century* (Boston: Houghton Mifflin, 1976), 150.

3. Jared Sparks, ed., *Writings of George Washington* (Boston: Little, Brown, 1848), 12:283.

4. John C. Fitzpatrick, ed., *Writings of George Washington* (Washington: Government Printing Office, n.d.), 5:460–61.

2. JOHN ADAMS

1. L. H. Butterfield et al., eds., *Diary and Autobiography of John Adams* (Cambridge, Mass.: Harvard University Press, 1961), 3:296.

2. Ibid., 1:246.

3. Ibid., 3:258.

4. Ibid., 2:28.

5. Ibid., 1:73.

6. Ibid., 1:79.

7. Ibid., 1:355.

8. R. Worthington, ed., *Letters and Other Writings of James Madison* (New York: published by order of Congress 1884, reprint of 1865 edition), 3:290.

9. Charles Francis Adams, ed., *Letters of John Adams Addressed to His Wife* (Boston: Freeman, 1876), 150–51.

10. Butterfield, 2:87–88.

11. Adams Papers, Massachusetts Historical Society: J. A. to Cotton Tufts, August 27, 1787.

12. Page Smith, *John Adams* (New York: Doubleday, 1962), 1:577.

13. Adams Papers, New York Historical Society: A. A. to Cotton Tufts, October 3, 1790.

14. Butterfield, 1:229–30.

15. Ibid., 1:247.

16. Ibid., 2:41.

17. Ibid., 3:228.

18. Ibid., 3:231.

19. Smith, 1:299.

20. Ibid., 2:1069.

21. Butterfield, 3:248.

3. THOMAS JEFFERSON

1. James Bear Jr., ed., *Jefferson at Monticello* (Charlottesville: University Press of Virginia, 1967), 18.

2. Jefferson Papers, Library of Congress: T. J. to Madame Noailles de Tessé, January 30, 1803.

3. Edwin Morris Betts and James Bear, Jr., eds., *Family Letters of Thomas Jefferson* (Columbia: University of Missouri Press, 1966), 400.

4. Andrew A. Lipscomb and Albert Ellery Bergh, *Writings of Thomas Jefferson* (Washington: Thomas Jefferson Memorial Association of the United States, 1903), 13:78–79.

4. JAMES MADISON

1. Madison Papers, New York Public Library: J. M. to Horatio Gates, March 10, 1802.

2. Saul K. Padover, ed., *The Complete Madison* (Millwood, N.Y.: Kraus Reprint Co., 1971), 324.

3. Andrew A. Lipscomb and Albert Ellery Bergh, *Writings of Thomas Jefferson* (Washington: Thomas Jefferson Memorial Association of the United States, 1903), 8:204–6.

4. Jefferson Papers, Library of Congress: T. J. to J. M., June 29, 1793.

5. Ibid., Joseph Dougherty to T. J., May 15, 1809.

6. Ralph Ketchum, *James Madison: A Biography* (Charlottesville: University Press of Virginia, 1990), 216.

7. Margaret Bayard Smith, *The First Forty Years of Washington Society*, ed. Gaillard Hunt (New York: Ungar, 1965), 233.

5. *JAMES MONROE*

1. Paul Leicester Ford, ed., *Works of Thomas Jefferson* (New York: Putnam, 1904–5), 8:223.

2. Andrew A. Lipscomb and Albert Ellery Bergh, *Writings of Thomas Jefferson* (Washington: Thomas Jefferson Memorial Association of the United States, 1903), 11:211.

6. *JOHN QUINCY ADAMS*

1. Charles Francis Adams, ed., *Memoirs of John Quincy Adams* (Philadelphia: Lippincott, 1875), 7:291.

2. Ibid., 8:545.

3. Ibid., 7:121.

4. Ibid., 7:255.

5. Ibid., 7:292.

6. Jack Shepherd, "Seeds of the Presidency." *Horticulture*, January 1983, 42.

7. Adams, 7:288.

8. Ibid., 7:323.

9. Shepherd, 40.

10. Adams, 8:23.

7. ANDREW JACKSON

1. John Spencer Bassett, ed., *Correspondence of Andrew Jackson* (Washington: Carnegie Institution, 1923–33), III:274.

2. *American Historical Magazine* IV:238.

3. Bassett, V:466.

8. MARTIN VAN BUREN

1. Charles Ogle, "Speech of Mr. Ogle of Pennsylvania on the Regal Splendor of the President's Palace," *Congressional Globe*, April 14, 1840.

2. John Niven, *Martin Van Buren: The Romantic Age of American Politics* (New York: Oxford University Press, 1983), 486.

9. INTERIM, 1841–50

1. K. Jack Bauer, *Zachary Taylor: Soldier, Planter, Statesman of the Old Southwest* (Baton Rouge: Louisiana State University Press, 1985), 108.

10. MILLARD FILLMORE

1. Charles Ogle, "Speech of Mr. Ogle of Pennsylvania on the Regal Splendor of the President's Palace," *Congressional Globe*, April 14, 1840.

2. Andrew Jackson Downing plans, National Archives.

15. THEODORE ROOSEVELT

1. *Theodore Roosevelt: An Autobiography* (New York: Macmillan, 1913), 328.

18. AFTER FDR

1. For a detailed account of the genesis of the Rose Garden, see *White House History, Journal of the White House Historical Association*, vol. I, no. 1, 1983, "President Kennedy's Rose Garden," Rachel Lambert Mellon.

BIBLIOGRAPHY

Adams, John. *Diary and Autobiography of John Adams*, eds. L. H. Butterfield et al. Cambridge, Mass.: Harvard University Press, 1961.

———. *Letters of John Adams Addressed to His Wife*, ed. Charles Francis Adams. Boston: Freeman, 1876.

Adams, John Quincy. *Memoirs of John Quincy Adams*, ed. Charles Francis Adams. Philadelphia: Lippincott, 1875.

Ammon, Harry. *James Monroe: The Quest for National Identity*. New York: McGraw-Hill, 1971.

Geer, Emily Apt. *First Lady: The Life of Lucy Webb Hayes*. Kent, Ohio: Kent State University Press, 1984.

Horn, Stanley. *Hermitage: Home of Old Hickory*. Hermitage: Ladies Hermitage Association, 1968.

Hunt-Jones, Conover. *Dolley and the "Great Little Madison."* Washington, D.C. American Institute of Architects Foundation, 1977.

James, Marquis. *Andrew Jackson: Border Captain*. New York: Literary Guild, 1933.

———. *Andrew Jackson: Portrait of a President*. Indianapolis: Bobbs-Merrill, 1937.

Jefferson, Thomas. *Thomas Jefferson's Farm Book*, ed. Edwin Morris Betts. Charlottesville: University of Virginia, 1976.

———. *Thomas Jefferson's Garden Book*, ed. Edwin Morris Betts. Annotated. Philadelphia: American Philosophical Society, 1985.

Johnson, Lady Bird. *A White House Diary*. New York: Holt, Rinehart and Winston, 1970.

Leighton, Ann. *American Gardens in the 18th Century*. Boston: Houghton Mifflin, 1976.

———. *American Gardens in the 19th Century*. Amherst: University of Massachusetts Press, 1987.

Levin, Phyllis. *Abigail Adams*. New York: St. Martin's, 1987.

Malone, Dumas. *Jefferson and His Time*. 5 vols. Boston: Little, Brown, 1948–70.

McEwan, Barbara. *Thomas Jefferson: Farmer*. Jefferson, N.C.: McFarland, 1991.

Morris, Sylvia Jukes. *Edith Kermit Roosevelt: Portrait of a First Lady*. New York: Coward, McCann & Geoghegan, 1980.

Niven, John. *Martin Van Buren: The Romantic Age of American Politics*. New York: Oxford University Press, 1983.

Seale, Williams. *The President's House*. Washington, D.C.: White House Historical Society, 1986.

Smith, Margaret Bayard. *The First Forty Years of Washington Society 1906*, ed. Gaillard Hunt. Reprint. New York: Ungar, 1965.

Washington, George. *The Agricultural Papers of George Washington*, ed. Walter Edwin Brooke. Boston: Badger, 1919.

———. *The Diaries of George Washington, 1748–99*, ed. John C. Fitzpatrick. 4 vols. Boston: Houghton Mifflin, 1925.

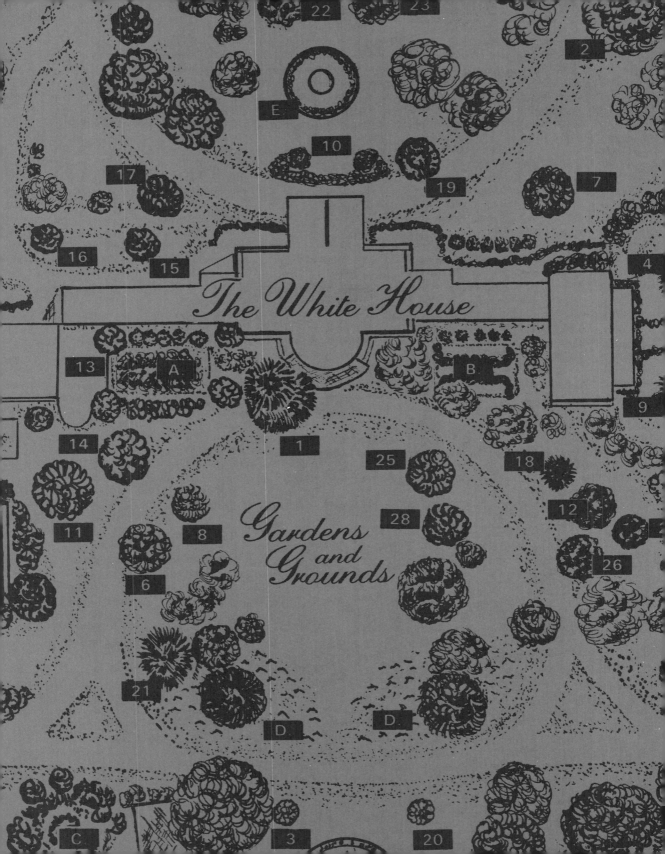

The White House

Gardens and Grounds